THE Gold Book
OF LESSON PLANS
Volume Two

TEACH
MAGAZINE · LE PROF

TEACH Magazine is dedicated to providing teachers with pragmatic tools and resources for classroom use. We have spent over 21 years developing curriculum-connected materials covering a wide range of topics and themes.

© TEACH Magazine 2014

Created in Canada

While extensive effort has gone into ensuring the reliability of the information in this book, the publisher makes no warranty, express or implied, with respect to the material contained herein.

ISBN: 978-09879018-7-3

Book font: Cicle and Century Schoolbook
Design by Kat Kozbiel

CONTENTS

PREFACE · iii

LESSON PLANS

LESSON ONE: Against All Odds · 1
Understanding the challenges and obstacles inherent in the refugee experience

LESSON TWO: The Canadian Studies Project · 11
An exploration of culture

LESSON THREE: History of Immigration · 39
An exploration of the experience of early immigrants who came to Canada

LESSON FOUR: My Commitment to Canada · 47
Understanding that citizenship endows certain rights, but along with those rights comes a set of responsibilities

LESSON FIVE: The Canadian Northern Project · 71
An exploration of the issues surrounding Canada's sovereignty in the Arctic

LESSON SIX: Welcoming Communities · 117
Pier 21 acted as a gateway to Canada for one million immigrants; this lesson plan tells their stories

PREFACE

We are presenting an impressive range of themes covered within the lesson plans that appear in this book. Themes such as human rights, the plight of refugees, interdependence and interconnectedness, how we feel about being Canadians, Arctic sovereignty and challenges in the north, the history of immigration and an exploration of the gateway to Canada for over one million immigrants; Pier 21.

You will find that the lessons are categorized by theme and grade level to facilitate simple navigation back and forth. Our wish is for you, the reader and user, to find what you need quickly and easily.

We know that teachers make do and even excel with what they have on hand; that resources can be scarce as well as expensive. TEACH Magazine is focused on accessibility and disseminating the learning resources we create as widely as possible.

This book is filled with substantive content. Based on pilot testing over the years, we also know that students want to have fun while they are learning. They want to be challenged and engaged. They want to know their voices are being heard and their viewpoints count for something. These are incentives for students to do their very best work no matter the theme or idea.

We at TEACH Magazine are confident we can help you, the classroom teacher, develop or enhance that stimulus for you students. They will have fun and they will challenge and be challenged as you work your way through each of the lesson plans contained in The Gold Book before you.

We are always open to feedback and insights that you may have.

Please feel free to contact us at any time: *info@teachmag.com*.

Enjoy the lesson plans we have provided.

Sincerely,

Wili Liberman, Editor

===== LESSON ONE

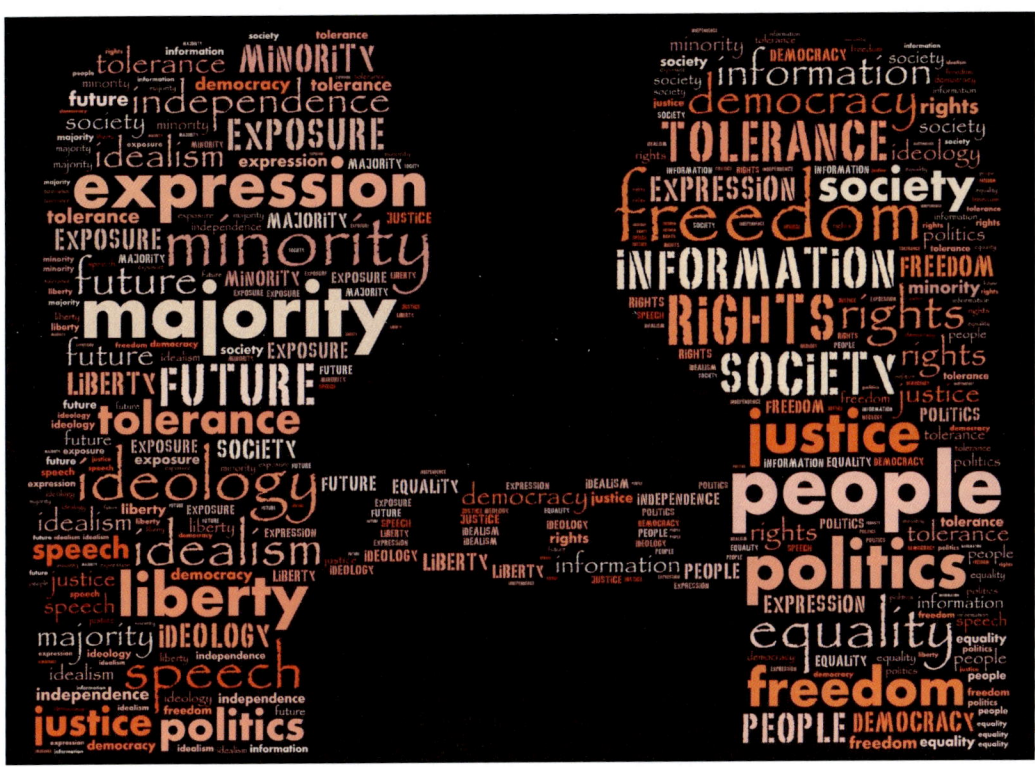

AGAINST ALL ODDS
EXPLORING THE PLIGHT OF REFUGEES
AROUND THE WORLD

The United Nations High Commissioner for Refugees (UNHCR) offers a free and significant resource to help teachers introduce the topic of refugees in the classroom. It is a game called Against All Odds (www.playagainstallodds.ca), an online simulation that allows students to experience the obstacles, terror, and choices people are compelled to make when they are forced to leave their homes and flee their country.

GRADE LEVEL:
7 – 12

CURRICULA
THEMES:

Language Arts,
Geography, History,
Political Science,
and Social Studies

INTRODUCTION

What do the following individuals have in common: Nelson Mandela, Malala Yousafzai, Natan Sharansky, Alexander Solzhenitsyn, Mstislav Rostropovich, Aung San Suu Kyi, Ken Saro-Wiwa, Albert Einstein, Michäelle Jean, and Madeleine Albright? At one time, each was either a refugee, a prisoner of conscience and/or a political dissident and subject to human rights abuses. In the cases of Sharansky, Solzhenitsyn, and Rostropovich, they left their countries of origin (former Soviet Union) to settle elsewhere.

After nearly 30 years of imprisonment in his native South Africa, Nelson Mandela became that country's president and is considered its most important and influential public figure. Support for Mandela's release reached a fever pitch until the government finally caved in. Natan Sharansky was released by the Soviet authorities after a world-wide campaign, spearheaded by his wife, exerted pressure on the government. He immigrated to Israel and subsequently became the Minister of Housing in the government. Alexander Solzhenitsin wrote some famous books notably, Cancer Ward, The Gulag Archipelago and One Day in the Life of Ivan Denisovich, that starkly documented the repressive mechanisms of the Soviet state. Solzhenitsyn left Russia and immigrated to the United States. After the fall of the Berlin Wall, however, he returned to his native land where he continued to live until his death. Aung San Suu Kyi, the acclaimed democracy leader of the Burmese people and the 1991 Nobel Peace Prize winner, spent six years under house arrest where she was separated from her husband and two young sons. She was released from detention in July 1995 by the State Law and Order Restoration Council (SLORC), a repressive regime set up by the Burmese military Government in 1988. She was subsequently placed again under house arrest until her release in 2010. The poet, Ken Saro-Wiwa, was imprisoned by the Nigerian government. He was subsequently executed despite international protests by governments, human rights organizations, and outraged individuals.

Now, imagine tens of thousands of others whose names we don't know, whose faces we do not see, whose stories we do not hear. They are spread throughout the world in countries we read about in newspapers. We watch 30 second clips of horror on television and online that mention places such as Bosnia, Darfur, Rwanda, Afghanistan, Burma, Sri Lanka, China, and Syria among others. Some, the lucky few, are released from prisons or accepted as legitimate refugees by countries, such as Canada, that have more welcoming immigration and refugee policies. A great deal of work, however, goes on out of the public eye. Lobbying, letter writing campaigns, protests and vigils take place, among other activities, to put pressure on repressive governments to release prisoners of conscience. Education and awareness are great weapons in the ongoing battle to change draconian laws and attitudes.

In 1919, Fridtjof Nansen, a remarkable, scientist, adventurer and humanitarian, was head of the Norwegian delegation to the League of Nations. He was chosen to deal with a difficult situation: the repatriation of some 450,000 prisoners of war from twenty-six different countries. Nansen was so successful that in 1921, he was appointed the first High Commissioner for Refugees and immediately set to work resettling and aiding in the integration of millions of refugees. Nansen was awarded the Nobel Peace Prize in 1922. He died in 1930, but the legacy of his great work lives on in the United Nations High Commissioner for Refugees, which came into being in 1950 through a vote in the General Assembly of the United Nations. Its mandate is as follows: Provide refugees with "international protection... searching for permanent solutions... helping Governments and... private organizations to facilitate the voluntary repatriation of refugees or their assimilation in new national communities." Since it began, UNHCR has helped over 50 million refugees. It deploys 7735 staff as of 2012 around the world as UNHCR officers seek to provide protection and security for 33 million refugees. UNHCR is mandated to lead and coordinate international action to protect refugees and find solutions to refugee problems worldwide. The 1951 Refugee Convention and its 1967 Protocol relating to the Status of Refugees are the foundation of its work to help and protect the world's refugees. While the primary purpose is to safeguard the rights and well-being of refugees, UNHCR's work has expanded to include other vulnerable groups such as the internally displaced and stateless people. They are working in 126 countries and help an estimated 32.9 million persons, with an annual budget of more than US $4.3 billion in 2012.

Throughout this teaching unit, you and your students will explore issues that relate to refugees and the conditions and crises that cause displacement using the game, Against All Odds, as a tool and resource. Integrated into this unit are the following curriculum areas: Language Arts, Geography, History, Political Science, and Social Studies.

LEARNING OUTCOMES

Students will:
- Understand the challenges and difficulties encountered by refugees, in part by experiencing the online game, Against All Odds
- Gain knowledge and insight on how to establish a new life in a different country
- Explore the history and significance of the concept of asylum
- Understand the importance of human rights
- Recognize Canada's role in human rights and refugee issues
- Understand how Canada's immigration system and method for resettling refugees functions
- Learn about the United Nations High Commissioner for Refugees and the respective mandates, goals, and objectives
- Gain insight into how UNHCR makes a difference by participating in the process as set up by Against All Odds
- Appreciate what Canada, as a country, has to offer when compared to others around the world

CLASSROOM ACTIVITIES

Introduction

MATERIALS:

Pens, pencils, notebooks, markers, and drawing paper
Computers, tablets, or devices with Internet access that can load Flash websites

DURATION:

Two to Four classroom periods

Against All Odds (*www.playagainstallodds.ca*) is broken down into three major elements: War and Conflict, Borderland, and A New Life. Each section represents a phase in the refugee experience and requires quick thinking, resourcefulness, and a little bit of luck to be successful, whether it's playing the game or living the actual events of a refugee. Within each element are subsections as follows: War and Conflict: Interrogation; You have to flee; Get out of the town; You have to leave the country now.

Borderland: Shelter for the night; Find the interpreter; Refugee or Immigrant?; New kid in the class.

A New Life: Looking for a job; Time to go shopping; Sort by origin, Your first apartment.

For players to advance from one element to the other, they must be quick on their feet and make sound choices. Make an incorrect choice and the consequences can be severe. Players will see and clearly understand the stark choices and circumstances facing real refugees.

To support the game and the players, there are two additional sections on the Against All Odds website. There are Webfacts that contains stories and videos providing real-life accounts of refugees in different parts of the world. There is also the For Teachers section that has details and information on corresponding resources available in Canada and elsewhere.

Brainstorm

Use the following definition of a refugee as a point of reference for the ensuing class discussion and exploration. A refugee is defined as "a person who, owing to a well-founded fear of being persecuted for reasons of race, religion, nationality, membership of a particular social group or political opinion, is outside the country of his or her nationality and is unable or, owing to such fear, is unwilling to avail himself or herself of the protection of that country." The four main elements of this definition are: well-founded fear, persecution, reasons of race, religion, nationality, membership of a particular social group or political opinion and outside the country of origin.

Begin with a class discussion about human rights. How do students view human rights? What does it mean to them? Make a list on the board of all the rights and freedoms students feel they are accorded in Canadian society. Are there any surprises in the suggestions? Take a few days and have students clip articles from newspapers, magazines or online that describe conditions in other countries. Have those articles brought in. Refer to the original list and compare their perception of rights in Canada to countries mentioned in the articles. After the comparison has been made, discuss the implications of each list. What does the list say about each of the countries? Have students write a short essay about why Canada is or isn't a good place to live based on the prior lists. Read the essays out loud and discuss the points of view of the class members.

In the above discussion, the idea of asylum may have come up or been introduced. To complete the discussion, explore your students' thoughts about the concept of asylum and what it means. Can they think of specific instances they know of, either personally or from history, where someone was given asylum? How important is it? What significance does asylum have when assessing the moral fabric of a person or a country? Have students make a list of situations where an individual or group might require asylum. Have them list too, who is capable of granting asylum. Is it a person, an institution or a country, or all three?

Have students then examine the definition of a refugee and determine whether the criteria apply to anyone they know or read about in the articles they may have clipped. For example, would the definition apply to such persons as Malala Yousafzai, Albert Einstein; Alek Wek; Michaëlle Jean; Salman Rushdie; Bangladeshi feminist writer, Taslima Nasreen; former Philippine President Corazon Aquino, or Rigoberta Menchu? Students must be able to justify their answers by referring to the definition.

Ancient Beginnings

Students will complete at least two of the following:

1. Read the following quote from the Greek play, Oedipus at Colon by Sophocles:

   Theseus: *"Poor Oedipus, tell me what you are seeking in coming to this city, and what you are asking of me. What terrible things you would have to tell me, in order for me to deny you my help. Like you, I remember, that I grew up in the home of others and in a foreign land I faced deadly dangers. So that, whoever asks my hospitality as you do now, I would not know how to turn away. In future you will stay here in safety, like me."*

   Who were Oedipus and Theseus? Why is Theseus saying this? And how is it he understands the situation in which Oedipus finds himself? What does this say about ancient Greek society? Write a short essay.

2. Abraham is considered the father of the Hebrews and also a Muslim prophet. When he was very old, his wife, Sarah gave birth to a son, Isaac. From Isaac,

descended all the tribes of the people of Israel. What were the circumstances that led to Isaac's birth? How was it a reward for a selfless deed? What might have happened if Abraham hadn't acted selflessly? Write a story based on this scenario.

3. Who were the Huguenots? What is their story and what circumstances forced them to flee their homelands? Write a story as if you were one of a family that fled to a new home. Write about your experiences and what happens to you and other family members. Make the story as realistic and detailed as possible.

4. Dante Alighieri was a famous Italian writer. In the year 1300, he was elected to the post of Prior of the Republic of Florence. Later on, he was forced to leave by the French. He moved to and wandered through the regions of Tuscany, Lombardy, and Romagna. What great works of literature did he write? Is it possible to determine what impact leaving a place he dearly loved had on his work? Write a brief essay exploring this theme.

5. Many peoples have fled their homelands as a result of military conquest. Choose one of the following and research and write a report about what happened to them. They are: the Maya of Guatemala, the Dinka people of Sudan, the Kurds, and the Tutsis of Rwanda, or one of your choice.

6. Profile one of the following refugees: José Artiga, Albert Einstein, Anna and Sigmund Freud, Leon Trotsky, Sitting Bull, or Aeneas. What happened to them? Did their experiences influence others? If so, how?

GAME ACTIVITIES

Students will play *Against All Odds* (www.playagainstallodds.ca) and:
1. In the War and Conflict section of *Against All Odds*, how does the game convey the feeling of fear and intimidation by the authorities? What specific elements of the game made this seem realistic? Students will write a short description about this section of the game concentrating on the choices the player is forced to make. Are these easy or difficult? And what are the consequences?
2. In the Borderland section of *Against All Odds*, what obstacles need to be overcome for a refugee to find his/her way to safety? List the hazards potentially encountered. How do you tell the difference between a refugee and an emigrant? Use the examples found in the game to explain this difference.
3. In the A New Life section of *Against All Odds*, what are the challenges facing a refugee living in a new land where they don't speak the language and don't understand the customs? List all of the obstacles that must be overcome. What is the best way to work constructively on these problems?
4. How does *Against All Odds* reflect on the refugee settlement programs in Canada? Do you think Canada is a welcoming country to refugees? If so, state your reasons why. If not, state the same.

RESEARCH ACTIVITIES

Students will complete at least two of the following:

1. What is the Universal Declaration of Human Rights? Who declared it and what does it mean? What effect has it had on refugees around the world? Does Canada recognize it? What effect has this Declaration had on Canadian laws and policies?

2. Define and describe the following with regard to the Canadian refugee system:
   a) The inland process;
   b) The overseas process.

   Approximately, how many refugees come to Canada each year? Every system has its strengths and weaknesses. Describe those of the Canadian system.

3. Over the course of a week, look for newspaper, magazine, and online articles that talk about refugees. Do an analysis on the coverage. How are the refugees and the situations in which they find themselves, portrayed? What impression does that leave with the reader? How could that impression be presented differently while still accurately reporting the story? What about the use of photographs? Were they appropriate? Did they go with the story? How might the photographs be used differently or another photograph used instead? Justify your reasoning and choices in the analysis.

4. Follow a similar process as in the previous question, except analyze broadcast news, either radio, television, pod or webcasts. If possible, record some clips from a broadcast and use those as the basis for your analysis. Write an analysis of the news coverage and justify your reasons and choices. How might the coverage be different? What about the use of video and audio clips? Were they appropriate and relevant to the story?

5. On the *Against All Odds* website, the Web Facts section lists the personal stories of a number of refugees, some of whom are known while others are not. Select two of those stories and profile each of the individuals featured.

CREATIVE ACTIVITIES

Students will complete at least two of the following:

1. Your school and community have decided to launch a campaign to publicize and raise awareness for refugees. Put together a team and develop a promotional effort to support the upcoming campaign. This might include developing advertising in various media such as, print, outdoor, radio, television and social

media. Divide up the responsibilities of the team members and assign tasks. You have just one month to research, write, produce and distribute the materials. You may want to tie the campaign into a larger community event like a conference or symposium, even a march or street parade.

2. Set up an in-class debate where the question is as follows: "Refugees place too much of an economic burden on Canadian Society." Choose the debating teams, one of each taking the pro and con sides. Have the teams do their research and prepare the presentations. The remainder of the class will judge who has won the debate.

3. The famous German playwright, Bertolt Brecht wrote the following: "I always found the name false which they gave us: Emigrants. That means those who leave their country. But we did not leave of our own free will, choosing another land. Nor did we enter into a land, to stay there, if possible, forever. Merely, we fled. We are driven out, banned. Not a home but an exile shall the land be that took us in. Restlessly we wait thus, as near as we can to the frontier, awaiting the day of return…." In addition to being a playwright, Brecht was a social critic who was forced to flee Nazi Germany in 1933. What did Brecht mean when he wrote these words? What is the difference between an emigrant and a refugee? In much of his work, Brecht explores the theme of alienation. How does his personal life and situation reflect this theme? Write a brief report and where possible, refer to specific examples found in Brecht's plays and writings.

4. One effective way that youth and community groups can make a difference is to adopt a specific case. Following is a sample letter that may be sent to the media, that is, local newspapers, radio and television stations, community cable channels and politicians, or shared through social media to publicize the plight of an individual or group. The sample letter concerns a young Mexican woman named Ruth Yudit Ortega Orozco. The letter is addressed to officials in the Mexican government:

"Your Excellency: I am writing to you out of concern for the safety of Ruth Yudit Ortega Orozco, a student leader and human rights activist who is apparently the target of a systematic campaign of harassment, abduction, and torture by members of the security forces. Ms. Ortega has been abducted twice, including an incident in Mexico City, where she was tortured, and both she and her family threatened with death. These threats have continued. After supporting street cleaners in a hunger strike to protect working conditions, she was told, "the Tabasco street-sweepers didn't die, but you will." Peaceful political activities should not put anyone at risk of torture and death. I urge you to ensure that she is protected from further abuses. I further call for an independent and impartial investigation into her abductions, torture and harassment, and that those found responsible be brought to justice.

Sincerely, …."

Look for other cases for students to adopt.

5. How does playing *Against All Odds* make the plight of refugees more meaningful and realistic? Students will deconstruct the game focusing on the elements that created a psychological and an emotional impact. They will describe how the game was effective in helping them understand the refugee experience. Included too will be a description of the technical elements such as the graphics and the audio; components that added a dose of realism. Why were these effects compelling and powerful?

6. Create a refugee scrapbook. This involves going out to the community and/or talking to other students in your own school. Document the experiences of those who have left their homelands. Be sensitive to their situation and needs, however. Perhaps they may contribute by writing of their experiences or adding photographs. Add to the scrapbook with your own writing about the process and what was discovered. Flesh it out with drawings, illustrations and photographs of those to whom you speak (remember, when taking photos to ask permission first). Contact local community groups who work with refugees and ask for their help and advice. Upon completion, present the scrapbook to the rest of the class. Perhaps, it could be part of a general display consisting of other scrapbooks or materials exploring the theme of refugees. If preferred, the 'scrapbook' can be created electronically using a scrapbook, photo, or video sharing app.

FINAL PROJECT

This teaching unit culminates in bringing a number of the strands together that have been explored up to this point. Launch an art exposition in your school with the theme, "The Canadian Refugee Experience—Through the Eyes of a Child." This means a number of things, that is, works of art created by students that reflects what they learned so far or explores a personal experience. Most often, it is women and young children most affected when upheaval causes the flight of a people. Thus, it is important to represent their experiences and search for meaning through creativity. The exposition could also consist of pieces submitted by refugees or refugee organizations to help promote and publicize the event. This might involve drawings, illustrations, collages, photographs, murals, posters, tapestries, to name but some. The exposition must be properly planned, implemented, and promoted. Turn it into a community event where anyone has the opportunity to view the work. Perhaps there's a local art gallery that might be able to assist. Alert the local media to generate as much exposure as possible. You might want to explore the idea of an online art exposition corresponding to the same theme. Works of art could then be posted to a website, blog, or social media for broader exposure. Schools from across the country and indeed, around the world might get involved and submit their own works for the "online exposition." Link this exposition to *Against All Odds*. Are there other creative ways, like online games and simulations that will help expose and explain the plight of refugees?

LESSON TWO

THE CANADIAN STUDIES PROJECT
AN EXPLORATION OF CULTURE, HISTORY AND INTERCONNECTEDNESS

The Canadian Studies project uses the Canadian Charter of Rights and Freedoms to launch an exploration into the rights and responsibilities we all enjoy as Canadians. These are values we are privileged to hold unlike others around the world. We begin with an examination of citizenship and citizenship rights. The lesson plan lays a foundation for understanding the demands of citizenship with a view to engaging students in a dialogue, one that will stimulate critical thinking and assessment. Within the content of the following lesson are activity-based tasks that students should find both challenging and stimulating.

GRADE LEVEL:
9 – 12

CURRICULA THEMES:

Civics, Drama, English, Environmental Science, Geography, Media Studies, Political Science, Social Studies, Visual Arts, World History

INTRODUCTION

"Canada is the greatest nation in this country."
— Former Toronto Mayor, Allan Lamport

We live side by side with our neighbors. If those neighbors are a province or two away, we are still close. The world has shrunk. It is connected. We can travel across the country within a single day. We can directly communicate in seconds from one end of the Earth to the other. In earlier, simpler times, sending a message could take days, months, and even years. Our interconnectedness is an asset.

When we live so close, it makes sense to get along. To get along, we need to communicate. To communicate effectively, we need to understand each other. Conflict arises through miscommunication which, in turn, leads to misunderstanding. These are simple and obvious truths. They are difficult to maintain and hold in place effectively.

"The die is cast in Canada: there are two ethnic and linguistic groups; each is too strong and too deeply rooted in the past, too firmly bound to a mother culture, to be able to swamp the other. But if the two will collaborate inside of a truly pluralistic state, Canada could become a privileged place where the federalist form of government, which is the government of tomorrow's world, will be perfect."
— Pierre Elliot Trudeau

The purpose of this resource is to deliver a practical tool to educators and high school students who will explore the concept of Canadian Studies through a series of detailed activities.

THE CANADIAN CHARTER OF RIGHTS AND FREEDOMS

In 1982, the Canadian Charter of Rights and Freedoms came into effect. It is one of the most significant pieces of Canadian legislation currently in existence. When immigrants were welcomed to this country before 1982, laws did not yet exist that guaranteed their freedoms, enshrined their rights and protected them from racism and discrimination. The Canadian Charter of Rights and Freedoms corrects this vital circumstance.

Guide to the Canadian Charter of Rights and Freedoms
http://laws-lois.justice.gc.ca/eng/const/page-15.html

What is the Canadian Charter of Rights and Freedoms?

The Canadian Charter of Rights and Freedoms is one part of the Canadian Constitution. The Constitution is a set of laws containing the basic rules about how our country operates. For example, it contains the powers of the federal government and those of the provincial governments in Canada.

The Charter sets out those rights and freedoms that Canadians believe are necessary in a free and democratic society. Some of the rights and freedoms contained in the Charter are:
- Freedom of expression
- The right to a democratic government
- The right to live and seek employment anywhere in Canada
- Legal rights of persons accused of crimes
- Aboriginal peoples' rights
- The right to equality, including the equality of men and women
- The right to use either of Canada's official languages
- The right of French and English linguistic minorities to an education in their language
- The protection of Canada's multicultural heritage

Before The Charter came into effect, other Canadian laws protected many of the rights and freedoms that are now brought together in it. One example is the Canadian Bill of Rights, which Parliament enacted in 1960. The Charter differs from these laws by being part of the Constitution of Canada.

Human rights and citizenship education in schools should be based on the following principles:

- The importance of reaffirming or developing a sense of identity and self-esteem
- Valuing all pupils and addressing inequality within and outside school
- Acknowledging the importance of relevant values, attitudes, and personal and social education
- Willingness to learn from the experiences of others from around the world
- Relevance to young people's interests and needs
- Supporting and increasing young people's motivation to effect change
- Citizenship education should be an ethos permeating all areas of school life

Why teach it?

- The world we live in is unequal and citizenship promotes the challenging and changing of this inequality
- We live in a diverse society, and citizenship gives youth the tools to counter ignorance and intolerance
- Citizenship enables the challenging of misinformation and stereotyped views that exist

- We live in an interdependent world and citizenship encourages us to recognize our responsibilities toward each other
- Citizenship is about flexibility and adaptability as well as a positive image of the future
- Citizenship acknowledges that we have the power as individuals; each of us can change things and each of us has choices about how we behave
- Teaching citizenship has a positive impact on students

Key Elements of Citizenship

Knowledge and understanding

- Social justice and equity
- Diversity
- Globalization and interdependence
- Sustainable development
- Peace and conflict

Skills

- Critical thinking
- Ability to argue effectively
- Ability to challenge injustice and inequalities
- Respect for people and things
- Cooperation and conflict resolution

Values and attitudes

- Sense of identity and self-esteem
- Empathy
- Commitment to social justice and equity
- Value and respect for diversity

Universal Declaration of Human Rights
www.un.org

On December 10, 1948, the General Assembly of the United Nations adopted and proclaimed the Universal Declaration of Human Rights. Following this historic proclamation, the General Assembly called upon all Member countries to promote the text of the Declaration and " to cause it to be disseminated, displayed, read and expounded principally in schools and other educational institutions, without distinction based on the political status of countries or territories."

All educators and youth should familiarize themselves with the following:

Do Citizens have rights? If so, what are they?

"...The General Assembly proclaims This Universal Declaration of Human Rights as a common standard of achievement for all peoples and all nations, to the end that every individual and every organ of society, keeping this Declaration constantly in mind, shall strive by teaching and education to promote respect for these rights and freedoms and by progressive measures, national and international, to secure their universal and effective recognition and observance, both among the peoples of Member States themselves and among the peoples of territories under their jurisdiction."

For example:

Article 1: All human beings are born free and equal in dignity and rights. They are endowed with reason and conscience and should act towards one another in a spirit of brotherhood.

Article 3: Everyone has the right to life, liberty and security of person.

Article 4: No one shall be held in slavery or servitude; slavery and the slave trade shall be prohibited in all their forms.

Article 5: No one shall be subjected to torture or to cruel, inhuman or degrading treatment or punishment.

Article 6: Everyone has the right to recognition everywhere as a person before the law.

Article 9: No one shall be subjected to arbitrary arrest, detention or exile.

In all, there are 30 Articles that comprise the Universal Declaration of Human Rights

With Rights, however, come Responsibilities:
- Understand and obey international laws
- Participate in democratic political systems
- Vote in elections
- Allow others to enjoy their rights and freedoms
- Appreciate and help preserve the world's cultural heritage
- Acquire knowledge and understanding of people and places around the world
- Become stewards of the environment
- Speak out against social injustice, discrimination and racism
- Challenge institutional thinking when it abrogates human rights

"Whether we live together in confidence and cohesion, with more faith and pride in ourselves and less self-doubt and hesitation; strong in the conviction that the destiny of Canada is to unite, not divide; sharing in cooperation, not in separation or in conflict; respecting our past and welcoming our future."

– Lester B. Pearson

ABOUT THIS RESOURCE

The purpose of this resource is to stimulate a dialogue among youth; to bring the idea of citizenship, multiculturalism and diversity into their consciousness. How can this be accomplished? Using this resource is a good beginning.

You will find four lesson plans for youth in grades 9-12 who are studying History and Geography and Civics as part of the curriculum.

The lesson plans explore the following thematic areas: Equity, Diversity, Peace and Interdependence.

Each lesson plan is activity-based, takes an integrated curriculum approach, lists resources, has clear goals and outcomes and provides an assessment and evaluation model.

The Process Outcomes in all lesson plans include:

- Working together in teams
- Sharpening critical assessment skills
- Focus on communication

Evaluation and Assessment criteria in all lesson plans include:

- Evaluating students' oral reports
- Assessing students' written work
- Evaluating students' individual and/or team presentations
- Student self-assessment of their team work

LESSON ONE: EQUITY

"In a world darkened by ethnic conflicts that tear nations apart, Canada stands as a model of how people of different cultures can live and work together in peace, prosperity and mutual respect."

— Former U.S. President Bill Clinton

DURATION:

One to Six class periods

KEY CONCEPTS AND ISSUES

This lesson plan explores the idea of Equity as it relates to ensuring that everyone in a given society has access to all the rights and freedoms available to them under the law without favoring one group over another.

OBJECTIVES/OUTCOMES

Students will learn:

- To appreciate the freedoms they currently enjoy and/or take for granted
- To recognize the different positions people occupy in a society or culture
- To assess challenges and determine solutions for those in inequitable situations
- To understand that many people on the planet live in difficult circumstances
- To deal with real world issues
- To work together in teams
- To sharpen critical assessment skills

Vocabulary List

Oligarchy
Junta
Consolidate
Autonomy
Caudillo
Estancia

Case Study

Juan comes from a family of small landholders in Argentina. He is now 18 years old and he came to Canada to live with relatives when he was 14.

Here is Juan's story:

Many families in the Argentinian countryside farm or operate ranches. And like many countries, there is a hierarchy of social classes in Argentina.

The elite are called "Caudillos", those who own large estates (estancias) throughout the land. For many years, the Caudillos ran the country as an oligarchy through much of the 19th and 20th centuries.

The Caudillos obtained their land holdings through royal grants or as a reward for being supportive of the government or ruler of the day. They controlled wages and contracts and as a result of their overall influence, the Caudillos influenced social, political and economic policies in the country. Not surprisingly, many of these policies favoured those in their own class. Comprised of cattle barons and merchants, the Caudillos, acquired more and more land squeezing out the smaller landholders like Juan's family.

Those opposed to the rule of the oligarchy and then subsequently the rule of the military style junta that came afterward, attempted to enact reform. They joined labour unions to help consolidate their influence, to see if they could make a difference in government policy that gave some control back to the smaller landholders.

The Caudillos realized their position was being threatened by the social activism of the smaller landholders and moved to neutralize this threat. Unofficially, this involved acts of violence against the leaders of the labour unions and those who spoke out against the Caudillos or challenged them for power.

Juan's father, Miguel was just such man. Miguel was afraid, but reasoned that he had no choice. If he and others didn't act, then their situation would only become worse. They'd never have any autonomy. They'd never be able to compete with the Caudillos and their monopolies or have the freedom to make their own decisions. The leaders of the protesters organized demonstrations to let the Caudillos and the government of the day know that the treatment they received was unfair and they were willing to do something about it. Sadly, their actions were met with a violent response. Some of the organizers were killed or simply disappeared.

As a teenager, Juan was denied many of the rights that North Americans take for granted. He wasn't able to attend school regularly, for example. He was needed to help out on the land. His family suffered financially because the Caudillos controlled the agricultural markets with the support of the government.

It is the goal of most parents to have their children progress, to realize educational opportunities; to get ahead in their careers and to do better financially. Juan felt like he was stuck in the same position as his father, that they would continue to labour on just to get by and never get ahead.

On the surface, Juan was faced with the most difficult situation of all: that of no choice; to simply continue as his father and grandfather had before him. Juan admired his father and felt that he was a brave man and feared for his safety. Fear seemed to be their constant companion as those who opposed the Caudillos suffered.

For his own safety and well-being, Juan's family sent him to live with an uncle and aunt in Montreal.

Step One: Reading and Discussing the Scenario
(1 Period)

Have each member of the class read the case study above, the story of Juan. Discuss the vocabulary words. Can they relate to his situation? If so, how? Is there anything that Juan's family could have done to change his situation? Remember this lesson is about equity and in the case study, one group is in control and the other is not. How could Juan's family have gained equity given their circumstances? Brainstorm some ideas. Have the class think about their own circumstances or those of someone they know. For example, perhaps someone belongs to a team or a club where they have no say in how it operates despite saying they would like to be more involved in the operation of this team or club. What can they do to change the situation for the better? After talking about these scenarios amongst themselves, can they apply what they have discussed to Juan's situation? Perhaps there are those in the group or the class who have come from a different country and can share their perspective on the equity in some of the relationships they have had or have currently?

Step Two: Creating an Action Plan
(1 Period)

Recall the brainstorming ideas from the previous period. Divide students into groups of three or four and have each group consider at least one of the following scenarios:

- Juan joins a youth movement in Canada, the mission is to lobby the Argentinian government to improve conditions for smaller landholders and give them more say in government policy
- Juan makes a presentation to the United Nations detailing the plight of his family and many others in his country; his story is picked up by the world media
- Juan concentrates on going to school in Canada to get a good education so he can improve his position eventually in society and help provide for his family

Keep the same small discussion groups. Have each group select one of the scenarios they consider the best solution given Juan's situation. The group will then present a brief oral report to the rest of the class laying out the reasons for their selection. Make a list of the suggestions in each report and write them on the board for everyone to read. After which, reintroduce the concept of equity.
- Do the student responses explore this idea?
- Are the suggestions realistic and doable for someone like Juan?
- It is also permissible for the group to come up with alternative scenarios

for Juan should they choose to do so. Again, their reasoning must be justified in the oral report to the class.
- Discuss how these scenarios can apply in a number of contexts. That is, to the students personally, to an organization to which a student may belong, to the situation of a particular group or culture and to a given country students may have read about or heard about in the news.

Step Three: Clarifying Inequality
(1 Period)

Once again, divide the students into small groups of three or four. Each group will devise a scenario that clearly demonstrates the level of equity in a given relationship. It might be a parent and a child, a worker and a supervisor, boyfriend and girlfriend, a new immigrant and a government official, a coach and a player and so on.

The team will devise a short script, fleshing out the situation. The scenario students create may have two to four characters in it. The group will rehearse either "acting out" or "reading out" the scenario for presentation to the class. After each performance, a few minutes should be allotted for response from the audience. Was the situation clearly presented? Were the "characters" believable and the circumstances realistic? Was there a resolution to the situation? Each presentation should have a duration of roughly five minutes.

Step Four: A Second Action Plan
(1 Period)

Write the ending to Juan's story. What actions does he take and what resolutions appear realistic and plausible. Refer back to Step One of the lesson for reference. Once the story is written, have the class form into small groups and have each member of the group read their story to the others. Have the group select one of the stories and present this story to the rest of the class, i.e., read out loud. The story should take about five minutes to read. Leave time for class discussion over each story read. All written stories are to be handed in to the teacher.

OPTIONAL EXTENSION ACTIVITIES
(1-2 Periods)

Students will complete at least one of the following:

1. Review the Canadian Charter of Rights and Freedoms. Is there an article within the Charter that most applies to Juan's situation? If so, write a short essay detailing how this aspect of the Declaration applies to Juan and if applied reasonably, might help improve his situation while in Canada and if he still lived in Argentina.
2. Consider the nature of equity in the following relationships:

- Members of opposing football teams
- Single mothers on welfare and social workers
- A Chief Executive Officer and assembly line workers
- Family farmers and corporate farms
- A married couple
- Canada and the United States

Choose one and describe in a short report the nature of the relationship and what sort of equity is present in that relationship between the two parties. Back your reasons up with concrete examples. Length: half page to a maximum of one page.

ASSESSMENT AND EVALUATION

Evaluate the class teams on their oral reports

Suggested criteria:
- Content (was the content/strategy clearly articulated and well thought out? Were the points the team made persuasive?)
- Presentation (was the presentation well-delivered, easy-to-hear and understand with good vocal quality, gestures, postures etc?)
- Effectiveness (were the points presented effective, how practical were the suggestions?)
- Teamwork (did the group work well and effectively together?)

Assess students on their written work

Suggested criteria:
- Grammatically correct with sentences properly structured, i.e., use of complex sentence structure and correct verb tenses, spelling and punctuation
- Comprehension of the word/phrases—sentences clearly reveal the meaning
- Ideas are expressed clearly
- Information is well organized.

Evaluate students on their presentation work

Suggested criteria:
- Present information clearly
- What have they done to enhance the presentation
- Effective use of oral and visual communication?

Student self-assessment of team work

Suggested criteria:
- Contribution to group knowledge
- Preparation undertaken for research and investigation
- Articulating goals, devising alternate solutions, selecting best alternatives
- Setting personal goals for working effectively with others

LESSON TWO: DIVERSITY—GETTING ON OR OFF THE BUS

DURATION:

One to Six class periods

We have it all. We have great diversity of people, we have a wonderful land, and we have great possibilities. So all those things combined there's nowhere else I'd rather be.
– Bob Rae, Former Premier of Ontario

KEY CONCEPTS AND ISSUES

This lesson plan explores the theme of diversity from the perspective of recognizing that differences equal strengths. That seeing and understanding these qualities is vital to accepting differences in others. Understanding differences leads to knowledge and insight into other cultures and experiences whether one interacts with an individual or a group.

OBJECTIVES/OUTCOMES

Students will:
- Learn to accept differences in others
- Gain insight into other cultures and experiences
- Reaffirm their own cultural identity while learning from others
- Work together in teams
- Hone their communications skills
- Critically assess situations and events
- Benefit from real world experiences

CASE STUDY: GETTING ON THE BUS

Maya is planning her first cross-Canada vacation. She is travelling with a group from her high school to each of the provinces and territories. She is very excited because this is the first time she is going somewhere on her own without her family. Maya is doubly excited about this trip for another reason. During the year, her English class developed an online communities project with schools across the country. This project involved creating a global campaign for the purpose of publicizing the dangers of landmines in war torn communities around the world. Maya's class connected with other classes and in particular, she became good friends with Sean from Cornerbrook, Lise from Trois Rivières, Roberto from Edmonton, and Sasha from Vancouver. The five of them are linking up in Halifax and Maya will meet her online friends face-to-face for the first time and they will travel together with the group for six weeks. During the course of the landmines project, Maya exchanged personal information with her new friends. They found out that her parents are originally from Trinidad and emigrated to Canada just before she was born. Her mother's family is originally from India while her father is a native-born Trinidadian. Sean's grandparents came from Pakistan and emigrated to Newfoundland in the 1960s. Lise's mother's family emigrated to Quebec from South Vietnam in the early 1970s. Sasha's family hailed from the north of Italy, very close to the border of the former Yugoslavia. After the Second World War, Sasha's grandparents moved to Florence, where she was born and when she was three, they came to Canada. Roberto's family is pure Catalan, the region around Barcelona, and dates back many generations. He was six when his family moved to Edmonton.

Maya and her new friends have a number of things in common. They are all the same age, speak English and love the idea of travelling across Canada to see and understand how the country works and seek different experiences. They all like the idea of being exposed to new things and embrace the spirit of adventure. They all come from different cultures and backgrounds however, and this means that some miscommunication is always possible. Each has a background that is shaped by specific customs, conventions, ideals, and manners.

For example:
- Sean is a Muslim and does not drink alcohol or eat pork
- Lise, Sasha and Roberto are used to having wine with their meals even though, technically, they are under age
- Roberto is a smoker and feels this is okay because it is readily accepted in his culture
- Maya plays on her school basketball team, but the others don't care for the game
- Sean and Roberto are huge soccer fans, but Maya and Lise aren't interested
- Sean prays five times per day and carries a prayer rug with him on the trip
- The others aren't particularly religious and don't attend services on any regular basis even though Roberto says his grandparents are strict Catholics
- Maya has a strict curfew when she is at home, but Lise and Roberto can stay out as late as they like even on weekdays
- They all like different types of food and different music, but share an interest in hip hop music

The following are some sample scenarios that Maya and her friends encounter on their trip:
- Roberto sits at the back of the bus and smokes, even though others around him object
- Sean interrogates every waiter in every restaurant to ensure he is not breaking any of the laws governing food by eating pork
- Lise and Roberto and Sasha regularly stay out after curfew because that is what they are used to and they try to convince Sean and Maya to do the same, even though the tour company has rules against it
- The others find it disconcerting when Sean stops everything he is doing so he can pray, whether it is on the bus or in the middle of a tour
- No one else among her new friends likes or understands basketball and they also can't figure out why Maya is so obsessed with it just because she plays on her school team
- Sean is critical when he sees the others in situations where they or others

on the tour are drinking alcohol
- Roberto is always perfectly groomed and never wears short pants, which the girls think is very funny

Step One: Teacher-Directed Discussion
(1 Period)

Have students in the class read the above scenarios. Teachers should explore the concept of belonging and wanting to be part of a group. Each of the above characters has different ideas, attitudes and perspectives that shape their outlook and actions. Introduce the idea of "being on the bus" as a metaphor for fitting in and sometimes this is difficult to do when an individual interacts with a diverse group. The idea is to be open-minded and then figure out how all of the experience, knowledge and skills within the group can be harnessed to solve problems and challenges.

Spearhead a general discussion with the class about Maya's situation. What do students think? Do they feel that Maya will be able to accept the differences in her new friends and have an enjoyable trip? Perhaps members of the class have some experiences of their own they wish to share? Have they travelled under similar circumstances? Students share their comments and insights with the rest of the class.

Step Two: Creating an Action Plan
(1 Period)

Divide the class into groups of three or four. List the scenarios from Step One:

- Roberto sits at the back of the bus and smokes, even though others around him object
- Sean interrogates every waiter in every restaurant to ensure he is not breaking any of the laws governing food by eating pork
- Lise and Roberto and Sasha regularly stay out after curfew because that is what they are used to and they try to convince Sean and Maya to do the same, even though the tour company has rules against it
- The others find it disconcerting when Sean stops everything he is doing so he can pray, whether it is on the bus or in the middle of a tour
- No one else among her new friends likes or understands basketball and they also can't figure out why Maya is so obsessed with it just because she plays on her school team
- Sean is critical when he sees the others in situations where they or others on the tour are drinking alcohol
- Roberto is always perfectly groomed and never wears shorts, which the girls think is very funny

Each group will pick a scenario and discuss it among themselves. Give each group 15 or 20 minutes for discussion time. How would they respond to the situation? What positive strategies can students employ to mitigate the possibility of conflict. If there is conflict, how would they resolve it constructively? Each group will select a spokesperson who will summarize their discussion orally for the benefit of the rest of the class in a two-minute presentation.

In Period Two, the same groups will select another scenario, one they did not discuss originally. The members of the group have now become the official Bus Authority. This is the legal entity or legislative body that has jurisdiction over buses and what takes place on those buses and the people who ride the buses. As the official Bus Authority, come up with a legislative or legal solution to the scenario chosen. This might come from the result of a legal debate. It may involve the passing of a new piece of "bus" legislation. Or perhaps, using existing rules and regulations if the situation warrants it. Again, the groups will discuss the scenario they have chosen for 15 or 20 minutes. They will select a spokesperson who will present their legal/legislative solution to the rest of the class.

OPTIONAL EXTENSION ACTIVITIES
(1-2 Periods)

Step Three: Off the Bus

You may keep the same groups as before or divide the glass into new groups. Regardless, each group is still the official Bus Authority. Thinking about Maya and her friends as they travel across Canada, one of the group commits a transgression. The official Bus Authority must decide what this transgression is and describe how it violates Bus Authority rules. The transgression is serious enough that the individual who committed it, may be ejected from the bus. The Bus Authority will discuss the seriousness of the transgression. One member of the Bus Authority will present the situation to the rest of the class.

Step Four: A Second Action Plan

Working with the same groups, each will be divided in half. One half of the group will act in the role of advocate for the individual who committed the transgression. The advocates will defend the actions of the individual and make a case for their "client" to stay on the bus. The other half of the group will act as opponents of the individual. These people will state their reasons why the individual should be ejected from the bus. They will state their case detailing their reasons and in particular, how the actions of the individual have violated the laws of the Bus Authority.

Each group will make an oral presentation to the rest of the class. The groups will describe the situation and the potential outcome. Then, the advocates will state their case in favour of the individual and why they should be allowed to stay on the bus. The opponents will do the same, describing why the individual should be ejected from the bus. The class will then vote on which side stated their case in the most convincing way. Each side will have about five minutes to make their presentation to the rest of the class.

ASSESSMENT AND EVALUATION

Evaluate the class teams on their oral reports

Suggested criteria:
- Content (Was the content/strategy clearly articulated and well thought out? Were the points the team made persuasive?)
- Presentation (Was the presentation well-delivered, easy-to-hear and understand with good vocal quality, gestures, postures etc?)
- Effectiveness (Were the points presented effective, how practical were the suggestions?)
- Teamwork (Did the group work well and effectively together?)

Assess students on their written work

Suggested criteria:
- Grammatically correct with sentences properly structured, i.e., use of complex sentence structure and correct verb tenses, spelling and punctuation
- Comprehension of the word/phrases—sentences clearly reveal the meaning
- Ideas are expressed clearly
- Information is well organized

Evaluate students on their presentation work

Suggested criteria:
- Present information clearly
- What have they done to enhance the presentation
- Effective use of oral and visual communication?

Student self-assessment of team work

Suggested criteria:
- Contribution to group knowledge
- Preparation undertaken for research and investigation
- Articulating goals, devising alternate solutions, selecting best alternatives
- Setting personal goals for working effectively with others

LESSON THREE: INTERDEPENDENCE

"We peer so suspiciously at each other that we cannot see that we Canadians are standing on the mountaintop of human wealth, freedom and privilege."
—Pierre Elliot Trudeau

DURATION:

One to Six class periods

KEY CONCEPTS AND ISSUES

This lesson plan explores the concept of Interdependence, where the world in which we live grows smaller. More people inhabit this planet, more resources are depleted, we are instantly in touch with each other. We are connected through the air we breathe, the water we drink, and the images we see on the Internet. No nation can go it alone entirely. At some point in a nation's history, a cooperative relationship needs to be formed with a neighbor or a partner whether it's sharing resources or trading in goods and commodities, righting a grievous wrong or supporting the other against a perceived enemy.

OBJECTIVES/OUTCOMES

Students will:
- Understand the links between nations
- See that the natural world is extremely fragile
- Link human rights to responsibilities of global citizenship
- Comprehend the role technology plays in linking people together
- Figure out why, we as human beings, need to depend on each other
- Work together in teams
- Hone their communications skills
- Critically assess situations and events
- Benefit from real world experiences

CASE STUDY: NATURE'S REVENGE

Samsul is 15 years old and lives in the Ampara coastal region of Sri Lanka. He lives in a village where the economic base is fishing. Each day, the men head out in their fishing boats to ply their trade in the hope that the catch of the day may be plentiful enough for them to sell to the local markets and supply their personal needs as well. It is a difficult and precarious existence. The sea is often rough and there are storms. Boats can be damaged or lost. The boats themselves are expensive to buy and cost quite a lot to maintain, not to mention the price of fuel for the diesel engines. Samsul has left school and is now helping his father fish for a living. His father is grateful for the help and an extra pair of hands is very useful. When the men aren't fishing, they are darning their nets or making necessary repairs to their boats. Samsul enjoys working with his father and is proud of the fact that he his helping to support the family through his labour. And by supporting the family, he is, in a way, supporting the village as well. When the fisherman sell their catch, it means they have money they can spend in the village, to purchase goods from some of the local tradesman which, in turn, helps them support their own families. In this way, everyone in the village is interconnected. Each depends on the other for help or trade or barter. Because of this system, it means that everyone in the village knows everyone else. Sometimes, this can be a nuisance, almost too close as neighbours know each other's business and other intimate and personal details too. It also means that this co-dependant system that has been created in Samsul's village is fragile and vulnerable to collapse in certain extreme conditions.

Unfortunately, for Samsul and his fellow villagers, some of these conditions do exist. They have been caught in an ongoing political dispute for many, many years. Samsul's village is near a regional border. And this border has been in dispute for two decades as a rebel faction has been fighting the government for independence. Samsul and his fellow villagers have not taken sides nor declared their support for one side over the other. They try to keep their heads down and cooperate with everyone. Yet the dispute causes serious problems for the villagers. In the past, the village has been raided by the rebels and although they were treated well enough, many of their much-needed supplies were taken and no compensation was offered. Then, when government troops intervened and the rebels left, inevitably some of the villagers would be accused of aiding the insurgents. Once the government troops were satisfied, this wasn't the case, and felt the area was secure enough, they, in turn would leave, opening the door to the rebels once again. And so it went on. In some ways, the villagers became accustomed to the comings and goings of the various factions and troops and stuck to the business and life of the village as best they could.

Within the space of just a few minutes on a particular day, however, this all changed. Far out in the Indian Ocean, a massive earthquake erupted deep below the surface of the water. This earthquake registered on seismographs around the globe at roughly 9.0 on the Richter Scale. The scale only goes up to ten. The cataclysmic force of the earthquake created a gargantuan disturbance in the water above the Earth's surface resulting in a gigantic tidal wave, otherwise known as a tsunami. On the surface of the Indian Ocean, the scope and breadth of the tsunami was almost unparalleled stretching for hundreds of kilometers and gaining heights of 10 meters or well over 30 feet. What's more, the tsunami was rapidly advancing toward coastal regions across the Indian Ocean.

On that morning, Samsul and his father were delayed from going out in their fishing boat as they were repairing some of their nets. What saved them was the fact they were in the boat when the gigantic wave swept down on their coastal village. The tsunami took them by surprise, there was no warning, and no reason for them to be alarmed. They did not know about the earthquake in the Indian Ocean. No alarm had been sounded because no warning system was in place. The tsunami swept in. The fishing boat broke its moorings and was carried up on the shore and inland for some 200 metres and then was pulled back almost another 100 metres before the water receded enough so the boat was left on somewhat dry land. Samsul had been too terrified to scream or cry out. He had been numbed with fear and could only hang on and watch with horror. By the time, the devastating waters had receded, Samsul's village had disappeared.

Vocabulary List:

Vulnerable
Cataclysm
Tsunami
Seismograph
Richter Scale
Unparalleled
Faction
Recede
Insurgent

Step One: Teacher-Directed Discussion
(1 Period)

Have students read Samsul's story and then have a general discussion of his situation. Focus the discussion points on various aspects of interdependence. That is, frame the discussion so that it explores a number of themes: Environmental Interdependence, Economic Interdependence, Human Interrelationships, Political Relations, Links to Resources. You may wish to break the class into groups of three or four students and assign each group one of the aforementioned topics to be discussed in more specific terms. What do students think about Samsul's situation? How do they think he can be helped and by whom? Has anyone in the class been in a comparable situation and if so, what did they experience? What do they think of the political context and what impact might that have on Samsul's situation over the longer term. Write the vocabulary list on the board. You may assign one word for each group to define and apply to the situation as detailed in the case study. Each group will report back on their discussion and the definition they've found for the assigned word.

Step Two: Creating an Action Plan
(1 Period)

Samsul's village and the region in which he lives has been declared a disaster zone. Many people have been killed or are missing. The remaining villagers have no resources and no means of repairing the damage that has been done to the area.

Divide the class into small groups (as above) and have each group come up with a general strategy for dealing with Samsul's situation and that of his village. This can be organized from the perspective of the local government, the regional or national government in that area. It can be discussed as if the group was a foreign government offering help and support or might be discussed as if the group was a prominent aid organization that was mobilizing its resources to help out. One member from each group will present the general strategy to the rest of the class.

OPTIONAL EXTENSION ACTIVITIES

Step Three: Building on the Action Plan
(2-3 Periods)

Keeping the same small groups as in Step Two, students will delve into the subject of interdependence in a more substantive way. Each group will use Samsul's situation as a start point but will select a topic from the following list: The Environment, Technology, Human Rights, Trade, War and Conflict, Peacemaking, the Media, Arts and Culture, and Poverty.

The group will then discuss their topic in the context of interdependence and make a list of factors. For example, in a disaster zone such as the one in Samsul's village, human rights need to be respected. That is, what is left of an individual's property and possessions should be left alone. There shouldn't be any looting. Government officials should offer aid and comfort. Neighbours should help each other. Foreign governments and organizations working in the region should provide support and resources to help improve the situation while recognizing that people in distress, although now impoverished, still retain all the rights they had before the disaster struck. Similarly, what factors affect environmental degradation and how do we as humans depend on clean air, clean water and healthy plant and animal life? How does technology link us all together so that we are truly part of a global village? These are some starting points for a few of the topics.

Once the group has figured out the list of factors that affect the topic they've selected, they will make a collage choosing images from newspapers, magazines, images from the Internet, etc. to illustrate the key elements that reflect interdependence. In addition, the group will provide a brief written description of the collage that supports all the main points they discussed earlier. Each group will then present their collage to the rest of the class.

Step Four: The Declaration
(1-2 Periods)

There are many declarations that exist in the world. In the United States, there is the Declaration of Independence. In 1948, the United Nations General Assembly tabled the Universal Declaration of Human Rights. In Canada, there is the Charter of Rights and Freedoms. Many nations and states have their own versions of declarations that address a wide range of issues and topics.

In recent years, a number of organizations have come up with Declarations of Interdependence. For an example of just such a declaration, please go to: *www.davidsuzuki.org/about/declaration*. You will find a description of just such a declaration made by members of the David Suzuki Foundation—a leading environmental organization. This is not the first such declaration, but it is one that is prominent. For a history of such declarations, do a search on the Internet using the phrase "declaration of interdependence."

Each student in the class will create their own, personal declaration of interdependence. This declaration may take the form of a poem, a rap song, a storyboard, a video, a website, a quilt, a collage, an animation, a sculpture, drawing or anything else someone wishes to use.

All of the declarations will be handed in to the teacher who may choose to display and/or feature all or some of them, so they may be shared with the rest of the class.

ASSESSMENT AND EVALUATION

Evaluate the class teams on their oral reports

Suggested criteria:
- Content (Was the content/strategy clearly articulated and well thought out? Were the points the team made persuasive?)
- Presentation (Was the presentation well-delivered, easy-to-hear and understand with good vocal quality, gestures, postures etc?)
- Effectiveness (Were the points presented effective, how practical were the suggestions?)
- Teamwork (Did the group work well and effectively together?)

Assess students on their written work

Suggested criteria:
- Grammatically correct with sentences properly structured, i.e., use of complex sentence structure and correct verb tenses, spelling and punctuation
- Comprehension of the word/phrases—sentences clearly reveal the meaning
- Ideas are expressed clearly
- Information is well organized

Evaluate students on their presentation work

Suggested criteria:
- Present information clearly
- What have they done to enhance the presentation
- Effective use of oral and visual communication?

Student self-assessment of team work

Suggested criteria:
- Contribution to group knowledge
- Preparation undertaken for research and investigation
- Articulating goals, devising alternate solutions, selecting best alternatives
- Setting personal goals for working effectively with others

LESSON FOUR: PEACE

DURATION:

One to Six class periods

"...Canada is rich not only in the abundance of our resources and the magnificence of our land, but is also in the diversity and the character of our people. We have long been known as one of the most tolerant, progressive, innovative, caring and peaceful societies in existence."

– George Radwanski and Julia Luttrell,
The Will of a Nation: Awakening the Canadian Spirit

"When the power of love overcomes the love of power the world will know peace."
– Jimi Hendrix

KEY CONCEPTS AND ISSUES

This lesson plan explores the idea of peace and how to achieve it, points to conflict resolution strategies and implementation, focuses on sources of conflict and how to avoid them.

Vocabulary List:

Emigrate
Social Welfare
Alienate
Ostracize
Antiquated
Antagonism

OBJECTIVES/OUTCOMES

Students will:
- Identify potential sources of conflict
- Learn how to defuse situations where conflict arises
- Understand the destructive nature of conflict in communities around the world
- Explore how to become a peacekeeping and peacemaking nation
- Critically assess information and seek solutions to real-world problems
- Work collectively in teams

Case Study

Monika and Michael attend the same school in Moncton, New Brunswick. They became friends in school, working on projects and studying together and are now a couple. Michael's family can trace their roots back hundreds of years. He is native-born. Monika's parents are Sikh and emigrated from India some twenty years earlier. Although neither of them is particularly religious, they cannot escape their origins. Monika's family left India to seek a better life for the entire family. Her mother is a lawyer and works for a community-based legal aid clinic while her father is an engineer and works for a software company.

Michael's father works as a welder for a company that manufactures small diesel engines. Michael's mother works in a hairdressing salon. Michael's parents understand the need for immigration, but are suspicious of foreigners feeling that they take advantage of the generous social welfare system in Canada and take jobs away from the locals.

Monika's parents are traditional and prefer that she "stick to her own community." Since she has been dating Michael, there have been many arguments and much tension in the household. Her parents don't approve of the relationship. They are afraid that the cultural gap is too wide for them to bridge and that they will be shunned by others in society, that as a mixed race couple, they will be ostracized, ridiculed and possibly attacked by those who hold hard line racial attitudes. At the very least, Monika's parents are afraid the young couple will never be accepted by either side and that they will remain alienated from everyone.

Michael and his father haven't got along for a number of years and he thinks his parents' attitudes are antiquated and narrow-minded. Michael doesn't care about culture or race, but he sees Monika simply as a person, one that he cares for. It hurts him that his parents don't see that and can't understand his feelings.

Monika and Michael feel, that in some ways, the antagonism they receive from both sides serves to strengthen their relationship and that if they are committed to each other, they can withstand, even win over both of their families. Nevertheless, it is difficult for them and has put a strain on their relationship.

Step One: Teacher-directed Discussion
(1 Period)

Have students read the story of Michael and Monika. What do students think of the relationship? Should the past have any bearing on what happens in the present? Do they think that Michael and Monika will stay together or that the pressure from both families will be too great to bridge the differences between them? Does their story remind students of any other famous couples?

Step Two: Action Plan
(1-2 Periods)

Write the Ending—Have students in the class write the ending to Michael and Monika's story. What do they think will happen to them? How will the relationship affect their respective families? As part of the preparation for the story development, students must include a separate character description and analysis of Michael and Monika. The descriptions may include a physical description, lifestyle choices, likes, dislikes, etc. Have students write the stories and hand them in. Maximum length: two pages.

The "Fight" List—Students will write out a list of things they get into fights, arguments, and disagreements over. This list may be comprised of things they've experienced with friends, siblings, acquaintances, strangers, parents, and other relatives. Form students into small groups and have them share their list with the group members. Each group will condense the list into the most common causes of conflict. Each group will appoint a leader who will read the list out to the class. The list will be jotted on the blackboard. From the most common situations listed, a master list will be compiled as the most common sources of conflict as identified by all the groups.

Acting on the Plan—Keeping the same groups, each will select one situation from the master list. The groups will devise a strategy or series of strategies designed to resolve the problem or the conflict. This strategy will be documented. Then the members of the groups will role-play the conflict in front of the other groups and apply the strategy they have devised. The rest of the class will give verbal feedback on the problem, the role-play and the strategy. Students should be prepared to discover that not all conflicts are easily resolved but may be made "manageable." That too, is part of the learning.

Some conflict resolution websites:

Mahatma Gandhi Foundation for World Peace: *www.gandhi.ca*
Conflict Resolution Information Network: *www.crinfo.org*
Conflict Resolution Network: *www.crnhq.org*

EXTENSION ACTIVITIES
(2-3 Periods)

Step Three: Another Action Plan

Images of Violence—Is violent behaviour influenced by what youth see in the media? Are these images merely a reflection of what happens in our society and the greater world or do these images encourage more violence? This is a debate that may never be resolved, but it is unquestionable that images of violence as seen in the media have some influence, if only on perceptions and attitudes rather than actions. Students will keep a journal for a period of a week and document any and all images of war and conflict they see and hear whether it's in the newspaper, on the radio, on television, websites, video games, or a video. Students will clip, download and/or photocopy as many images as possible and cite the source. Students will then select one or two of the most powerful images they have collected and write about how they can help us get to the root of violence and conflict. How can these images be used to understand why violence occurs and ultimately lead to a resolution of the conflict? Maximum length: one page.

Boys and Girls Together—Patterns of behaviour and conflict can be separated along gender lines. We know that boys tend to be more rough and tumble and naturally more aggressive. Statistics tell us that male youth have a higher incidence of physical conflict. That doesn't mean girls aren't violent at times, but it is predominantly a male phenomenon. Girls, however, do exhibit a different pattern and tend to get involved in more emotional or behavioral conflicts than boys. Girls tend not to act out conflicts physically.

Divide the class into teams where they will discuss this issue among themselves. Ensure there is a good gender mix on each team. Why do they think these different sorts of behaviours take place? Is there a way for boys to resolve problems without resorting to physical aggression or violence? Is it a matter of having more physical outlets for boys at school? In the community? What other factors are there? In school? At home? In the community? How can boys make an effort to prevent themselves and their family, friends, acquaintances from getting drawn into an incident that could lead to acts of violence?

The team will research this issue and come up with a detailed list of recommendations and strategies that will help deal with the issue of male aggression and conflict. Each team will make an oral presentation to the class using any visual aids they can such as video, PowerPoint, overheads, drawings, photographs, or a website to illustrate their approach and strategies.

ASSESSMENT AND EVALUATION

Evaluate students on their reports and written work

Suggested criteria:
- Write the Story, Images of Violence Reports (Was the content clearly articulated and well thought out? Were the points persuasive?)
- Grammatically correct with sentences properly structured i.e., use of complex sentence structure and correct verb tenses, spelling and punctuation
- Comprehension of the word/phrases—sentences clearly reveal the meaning
- Ideas are expressed clearly
- Information is well-organized

Evaluate students on their oral presentation work

Suggested criteria:
- Presented information clearly
- What have they done to enhance the presentation?
- Effective use of oral and visual communication

Evaluate students on their visual presentation work

Suggested criteria:
- Visually appealing
- Good use of materials
- Well thought out
- Clearly represents the subject

Student self-assessment of teamwork

Suggested criteria:
- Contribution to group knowledge
- Preparation undertake for research and investigation
- Articulating goals, devising alternate solutions and selecting best alternatives
- Setting personal goals for working effectively with others

LESSON PLAN RUBRIC
(applicable to all four lessons)

Format
(Of written and oral reports)

Level 1: Includes at least one concluding statement and rationale, but missing one or more background facts or some significant information.
Level 2: Includes all elements of a report including at least two concluding statements, a rationale and some background information.
Level 3: Includes at least three concluding statements with a logical rationale and good supporting and detailed background information.
Level 4: Includes at least four concluding statements supported by an excellent rationale and detailed, thoughtful, background information.

Content
(Completeness and research)

Level 1: Conclusion is present, but lacks significant supporting evidence in the rationale or background information. One source is used for research. The source is noted.
Level 2: The conclusions are clear, but may lack sufficiently researched background information. Two sources were cited and noted.
Level 3: The conclusions are clear and solid research is apparent tying into the rationale and background information. Three sources were used and credited.
Level 4: The conclusions were clearly expressed and thoroughly researched and connected to the rationale and background information. At least four sources were used and cited.

Effort
(Teamwork and individual contribution)

Level 1: One or two people dominated the group to the detriment of the team effort. Very little cooperation. The talents of individuals went unrecognized and underutilized.
Level 2: Most of the group made a good contribution. Some recognition of individual strengths but not used to best effect. Cooperation was superficial.
Level 3: Most team members made a significant contribution and everyone was involved. There was a good level of cooperation.
Level 4: Individual strengths were recognized and used effectively. Excellent cooperation with all members playing a significant role.

Presentation
(Written and oral, discussion and debate)

Level 1: The written report has many writing errors and is poorly structured, causing confusion. The oral report was also confusing, lacked emphasis and energy. No discussion resulted.

Level 2: The written report was generally clear, but had numerous writing errors. The structure was apparent but not effective. The oral report was clear but lacked energy or emphasis and provoked little discussion.

Level 3: The report was well-structured and clear but had a few significant errors. All parts were easily identifiable. The oral report was clear and well-presented but lacked some emphasis and energy but some good discussion ensued.

Level 4: The written report was very clear and well organized with few errors. The headings and all sections and sub-sections were clearly marked. The oral report and discussion were very clear and energetically and creatively presented in an organized manner.

= LESSON THREE

HISTORY OF IMMIGRATION
Understanding the challenges and hardships faced by early settlers to Canada

Canada, even before it was a country officially, experienced successive waves of immigration. Grosse île is an island in the St. Lawrence River roughly 46 kilometres downstream from Quebec City. Today, Grosse île stands as a monument to suffering and sacrifice, as well as a system that was ill-equipped to deal with the level of immigration it experienced and the difficulties rendered.

Image Credit: Louis Chamberland
Source: *www.chaudiereappalaches.com*

GRADE LEVEL:
10 – 12

CURRICULA THEMES:

History, Geography Civics, English, Language Arts, Visual Arts, Health and Well-Being

INTRODUCTION

Before the advent of commercial air flights, would-be immigrants boarded ships and sailed to their new destinations. With the collapse of the slave trade to North America, unscrupulous ship owners found a lucrative alternative in providing commercial passage to those leaving their homelands. The more passengers they could pack in, the more money the ship owners made. The cramped, unsanitary and airless conditions on board the ships provided the perfect breeding ground for disease, precipitating a series of epidemics, among the first brought to the shores of North America. Passengers were forced to endure up to 10 weeks of hellish conditions before reaching port.

Given the rising incidence of disease found among passengers travelling on these vessels, Grosse Île became a stopgap, a way station before any ships were allowed to sail closer to civilization and any passengers were allowed to disembark.

The event that triggered Grosse Île's transformation into a quarantine station, was a major cholera epidemic that broke out in 1832 where 51,746 Irish and English immigrants were examined. The disease had spread from Asia by passengers travelling west. Despite the quarantine, the disease managed to spread to Quebec City where 3,800 perished and to Montreal where 1,900 died in the following year. Not much was known about the disease then, or how to effectively contain it.

But that was not to be the worst of it. The year 1847 announced the Irish Potato Famine and droves of Irish immigrants fled starvation, all of which took place during a major typhoid fever epidemic. Ship after ship navigated the waters of the St. Lawrence only to be held back at Grosse Île. The medical authorities in charge of the quarantine station had no idea what was sailing their way. After a number of years of relative calm after the cholera crisis had ended in the 1830s, conditions had stabilized and the medical staff and volunteers were well enough equipped to deal with most situations at the time.

As successive ships arrived in the St. Lawrence, none were permitted to go through until they were declared disease-free. Ships with fever cases were required to fly a blue flag. Grosse Île soon found itself ill-equipped to deal with the sheer number of cases. Of the affected ships, passengers were required to stay on board for an undisclosed number of days. In some cases, doctors gave perfunctory examinations and allowed infected passengers to leave their vessels to spread the contagion elsewhere.

In relatively normal conditions, healthy passengers would have been kept in quarantine huts on the island while the sick were cared for in hospital. Because of the sheer numbers, this became impossible. Tents were set up as quickly as it was feasible, but many of the sick were left out in the open or stacked on wooden bunks. There was also a water shortage where the risk of dehydration led to a painful death.

In addition to other shortages, the numbers of qualified medical personnel were insufficient. And often, nurses, doctors, volunteers, even priests and clergymen succumbed to the spread of the disease. Most, if not all, of the afflicted came from the British Isles whereas other emigrants, such as the Germans, arrived healthy and disease-free. Even the so-called healthy passengers suffered from the privation inflicted on them due to the epidemic.

It is difficult to know how many actually perished in the epidemic as some bodies were buried at sea on the voyage over before reaching the St. Lawrence. Of all, Irish immigrants suffered the highest number of casualties. A monument to the Irish dead stands on Grosse Île, as does a cemetery where some 6,000 Irish men, women, and children are buried. The remnants of the quarantine station on the island remain today as evidence of its tragic history. Grosse Île is now a national historic site and national park. It is hard to imagine that almost 450 ships carried Irish immigrants to these shores and that medical personnel examined just over 90,000 passengers. At times, there were so many ships waiting to be cleared by authorities, that the line stretched over two kilometres. Some 25,000 immigrants were held on the island at one time while the crisis unfolded.

The quarantine station on Grosse Île finally closed in 1937. During the Second World War, secret bacterial research was conducted there and public access was closed off. The island then reverted to a quarantine site, but for animals. In 1983, the Canadian government declared Grosse Île a national historic site and it became a national historic park ten years later and operates under the authority of Parks Canada. In 1997, a memorial was erected dedicated to those who died on the island. The largest monument on the island is the Celtic Cross that stands some 15 metres or more in height and is dedicated to the Irish who perished there.

LEARNING OUTCOMES

Students will learn:
- Gain insight into the history of immigration in Canada
- Work with primary source digital documents, archives and objects
- Understand the sacrifices immigrants make when they leave their homelands to come to another country
- Explore the history of Grosse Île and compare the immigrant experiences of other groups that came to Canada
- Understand the reasons people seek to emigrate
- Appreciate the conditions and hardships immigrants faced
- Work cooperatively in teams
- Apply critical thinking techniques and processes
- Put themselves in the shoes of new immigrants

Step One: Teacher-led Discussion

Teachers will lead a general discussion about immigration and immigration issues. If there are those in the class who have family stories or have recently emigrated, then these histories should be shared with the class. Make a list of reasons as to why people leave their land of origin and move to a new place. List these reasons on the board.

Step Two: Research

Students will be divided into teams of three or four. Each team will select a communicable disease that has had serious implications for immigration and immigrants, as well as general populations. The teams will research the chosen disease and write a brief report. Choices of diseases include:
- Cholera
- Typhoid Fever
- Tuberculosis
- Chicken pox
- Diphtheria
- Rubella (German Measles)
- Influenza
- Plague
- Tetanus

The report will consist of a history of the disease, impact on the population, effects of the disease, whether it is treatable, how to prevent or avoid infection, and the consequences of not being treated. The report will be handed in to the teacher for evaluation. Maximum length: two pages.

Step Three: Connecting to History

The devastating effects of cholera and typhoid fever were experienced on Grosse Île roughly 150 years ago. This was not the worst epidemic in recorded history, however. There are historical reports of the Plague or the Black Death that swept through Europe and the British Isles and outbreaks of Bubonic Plague that were devastating. But none of these were the worst. That title belongs to the 1918 Influenza Pandemic known as the Spanish Flu outbreak at the tail end of the First World War. During the War, soldiers and civilians in conflict areas lived through horrific physical conditions, but this was not the cause of the pandemic. The massive mobilization of armies and people displaced, however, increased the rate of infection. The Influenza Epidemic is estimated to have affected roughly five per cent of the world's population and although no accurate numbers pertaining to the death toll have been recorded, it is thought that up to 100 million people died. There were many anomalies connected to this pandemic. In particular, it severely affected those aged from 20-40, just the opposite of common flu outbreaks that normally target the very young or the elderly whose immune systems are not as resistant to any given flu strain.

It has been dubbed the Spanish Flu as it was thought the epidemic originated in Spain, or at least, it was the first area recognized to have been stricken. Since then, however, it is thought that the flu pandemic actually originated on a military base in Kansas where chickens were raised. Forensic scientists have determined the flu pandemic has been identified as a type of avian flu that may have jumped from poultry to humans and was spread through direct contact. Given the massive disruption and mobilization of people at the end of the First World War, the disease spread rapidly across Europe, Asia, and North America. The impact of the H5N1 avian strain of virus was horrendous and some communities were almost entirely wiped out. Many of those stricken died within hours of exhibiting symptoms. Medical research was in its infancy in those days, and not much was known about the disease, how to prevent it, or how to treat it. Conventional quarantine and isolation strategies were ineffective due to the mass numbers infected, which included medical personnel and volunteers. The only remedy that appeared to have some positive impact was blood transfusions from recovered flu victims. But this was discovered too late to help most who were stricken.

Contemplating such a scene today seems like a science fiction scenario and fodder for alarmists. Yet there have been serious warnings and significant media coverage on recent bird flu outbreaks, most of which appear to have originated in China, but have spread to other countries and as far afield as the shores of the United Kingdom. Like the SARS crisis of 2003, the spread of infectious disease can be rapid. We live in a mobile society where the globe can be traversed in less than a day and the enclosed ventilation systems of airplanes provide opportune conditions for disease transmission. An individual with a highly infectious and drug-resistant strain of tuberculosis can take several flights between North America and Europe. When this happens, hundreds of passengers may be directly affected through exposure to the disease. These types of incidents can raise media firestorms.

Keeping the same teams, students will research and write a news broadcast where the situation involves the outbreak of a new pandemic. The team needs to convey clear information to their audience detailing what the disease is, its origins, how it can be contained, treated and/or cured, while documenting the immediate impact with specific stories or case histories of those affected. The stories should focus on those travelling or emigrating from one country to another as the primary source of transmission and spread of this new pandemic. The news broadcast may be presented live, video or audio recorded, and/or storyboarded. The class and the teacher will evaluate the effectiveness of the news broadcasts.

Step Four: Trace the Steps

Like Ellis Island in the United States and later on, Pier 21 in Canada and Grosse Île was meant to be a way station or clearinghouse for those wishing to settle in this country. Working in teams or individually, students will research the immigration history of a particular nationality, such as Italians or the Vietnamese. Where possible, bring individual stories to light to make the journey taken more personal. Look for archival materials that document direct experiences (the Canadian Museum of History has several online collections. Students can find links to them here: *www.historymuseum.ca/cmc/exhibitions/tresors/immigration/imf0000e.shtml*). Once the research has been completed, write up a brief report of the findings. Submit the report to the teacher. Maximum length: Two pages.

Step Five: Walk in the Shoes

Drawing on the research that was conducted for Step Four, students, working individually or in teams, will create a diary or a journal documenting the journey of an immigrant. The journal can be based on a real person discovered in the course of the research or a fictionalized character created for this activity. The idea is to bring to life the thoughts, perceptions, feelings and observations of an individual going through the life-changing event of leaving a homeland and settling in a new country. If desired, the journal can be augmented with sketches, illustrations, even objects or mementos to bring the journal to life. The journal entries do not have to be enormously detailed, but should cover a minimum two-week period in the character's life. The journal should also include a biography of the character that details relevant background information (e.g., age, gender, education, etc.).

Step Six: I, the Minister

It is the year 1920. The First World War has recently ended and the devastating flu pandemic has been brought under control. Student teams will take on the role of the Minister of Immigration. That is, what will the immigration policy for the new, emerging Canada be? Will the country welcome new immigrants or close its doors? Part of the policy document to be created will set out qualifying conditions to emigrate to Canada and what sort of future citizens the country requires. For example, will there be an emphasis on farmers or factory workers? Does the government want families or single men with a trade? What health screening will be required? Will any government services be provided to new immigrants and if so, what will they be? Once the policy is drafted, each team will present their document in "Parliament" (the class), to the members of the government, and the opposition. The government policy must be publicly released to members of the government and the public.

Once the document has been circulated and presented, members of the House of Commons (classmates) will have the opportunity to question aspects of the policy that is being tabled. Typically, new policies are sent off to various committees for discussion and study before making it through the process that is required to pass a proposed bill into law. The policy needs to be carefully thought out by each team and research completed so answers to questions may be provided. At the end of the discussion, the "parliament" can vote on the policy to determine whether the proposed policy has a chance of making it into law. And the vote will determine how successful the team has been in promoting their immigration policy.

Parliament of Canada Research Library
www.parl.gc.ca/information/library/PRBpubs/bp437-e.htm

Early Canadiana Online
http://eco.canadiana.ca

Officers and Officials of Parliament
*www.parl.gc.ca/Parlinfo/compilations/OfficersAndOfficials/
   ProceduralOfficersAndSeniorOfficials_Library.aspx?Language=E*

OPTIONAL EXTENSION ACTIVITIES

- Write and produce a storybook for younger children that tells the story of a young person's journey from their homeland to Canada
- Create an immigration symposium in the school to address specific issues around concerns immigrants have and invite guest speakers from the community
- Put on a heritage fair in the school or community that focuses on immigrant stories and history
- Build a public awareness campaign around specific issues of concern to new immigrants and invite the local media
- Examine current immigration policy and have a debate as to whether this policy serves the needs of the community or not
- Invite recent immigrants to the class and have them tell their stories

RESOURCES

www.En.wikipedia.org/wiki/Spanish_flu
www.En.wikipedia.org/wiki/cholera
www.En.wikipedia.org/wiki/typhoid
www.thecanadianencyclopedia.ca/en/article/la-grosse-ile
www.moytura.com/grosse-ile.htm
www.en.wikipedia.org/wiki/Grosse_Isle,_Quebec
www.ist.uwaterloo.ca/~marj/genealogy/papers/children1847.html
Island of Hope and Sorrow, The Story of Grosse Île, Anne Renaud,
   Lobster Press, 2007.

ASSESSMENT AND EVALUATION

Evaluate the class teams on their oral reports

- Content: was the content/strategy clearly articulated and well thought out? Were the points the team made persuasive?
- Presentation: was the presentation well-delivered, easy-to-hear and understand with good vocal quality, gestures, posture etc.?
- Effectiveness: were the points presented effective? How practical were the suggestions?
- Teamwork: did the group work well and effectively together?

Assess students on their written work

- Grammatically correct with sentences properly structured, i.e., use of complex sentence structure and correct verb tenses, spelling and punctuation
- Comprehension of the word/phrases—sentences clearly reveal the meaning
- Ideas are expressed clearly
- Information is well-organized
- Evaluate the groups on their presentation work:
- Is the information presented clearly?
- What have they done to enhance the presentation?
- Is the use of oral and visual communication effective?
- Evaluate students on their presentation work:
- Their contribution to group knowledge
- The preparation undertaken for research and investigation
- Articulation of goals, devising alternate solutions, selecting best alternatives

LESSON FOUR

MY COMMITMENT TO CANADA

AN EXPLORATION OF CITIZENSHIP RIGHTS AND RESPONSIBILITIES

The purpose of this resource is to help establish a dialogue with youth that will stimulate thought and debate about citizenship. More to the point, it is vital that youth become actively engaged in citizenship-based activities, to take an active role in their respective communities, to explore, to understand what it means to fully be a Canadian citizen.

GRADE LEVEL:
7 – 10

CURRICULA THEMES:

History, Social Studies, Citizenship, Global Citizenship, Civics

INTRODUCTION

Canada is a magnet for immigrants; one of the most multi-culturally diverse countries in the entire world. Canada houses the United Nations. For those who are new to our country, citizenship may mean everything. For the second generation and beyond, the importance of citizenship may get lost in the hectic scramble to succeed in school, at work, in life.

Youth must understand that citizenship carries rights in its pocket; with these rights come responsibility to participate in the community. Citizens bear the responsibility for helping to run the community; helping give the community its life and vigour. Any democratic nation is only as strong as its citizens. Without active commitment and participation, the community suffers and grows weak.

Canadian Citizenship delivers rights:
- Equality rights: equal treatment before and under the law, and equal protection and benefit of the law without discrimination
- Democratic rights: the right to participate in political activities, to vote and run for political office
- Legal rights: the right to be presumed innocent until proven guilty, the right to retain a lawyer and be informed of that right, and the right to an interpreter in court proceedings
- Mobility rights: the right to enter and leave Canada, to move and take up residence in any province or territory
- Language rights: the right to use either the English or French language in communications with Canada's federal government
- Education rights: French and English minorities in every province and territory have the right to be educated in their own language.

With rights come responsibilities:
- Understand and obey Canadian laws
- Participate in Canada's democratic political system
- Vote in elections
- Allow other Canadians to enjoy their rights and freedoms
- Appreciate and help preserve Canada's multicultural heritage

ABOUT THIS RESOURCE

How do we make active citizenship a relevant question for youth? How do we bring this idea into their consciousness? Using this resource is a good start.

The Final Activity will engage youth in the development of their own Charter or Declaration of Citizenship.

Each Lesson Plan and the Final Activity is activity-based, takes an integrated curriculum approach, lists Web-based resources, has clear outcomes and provides an assessment model.

The Process Outcomes in all lesson plans include:
- Working together in teams
- Sharpening critical assessment skills

Evaluation and Assessment criteria in all lesson plans include:
- Evaluating students' oral reports
- Assessing students' written work
- Evaluating students' individual and/or team presentations
- Student self-assessment of their teamwork

LESSON ONE: RESPECT

KEY CONCEPTS AND ISSUES

This lesson plan explores the idea of Respect as it relates to the law, the environment and each other

OBJECTIVES/OUTCOMES

Students will learn:
- To appreciate the environment
- To understand the differences between those of different backgrounds and cultures
- To understand and appreciate community values
- To be accepting of others even if we don't agree with their point of view
- To deal with real-world issues
- To work together in teams
- To sharpen critical assessment skills

CASE STUDY

Molokai emigrated from Somalia with his family ten years ago. Somalia then was a country devastated on many levels. It was split by catastrophic tribal warfare that saw at least 300,000 civilians die from violence or lack of adequate food and water. It is a country that is politically unstable and frequently suffers from terrible droughts. It is an arid land with little clean water. Due to the civil unrest, the country's infrastructure is fragmented and dysfunctional. Molokai was co-opted as a child soldier. His father and two of his brothers were killed in the ongoing struggles between the warring tribes. Finally, Molokai's mother, his sister, an aunt and an uncle were able to emigrate to Canada. Molokai is now 18 years old. He is in his second last year of high school. He didn't have the opportunity to go to school for a number of years because the schools were closed periodically in Somalia. Molokai and his family live in a high-rise building in the west end of Toronto. Many Somalis live there. Some call it an urban ghetto where the Somali immigrants have been warehoused to keep them out of the way. Some live there because they feel more comfortable with those from their own community who speak the same language and understand the culture and customs of Somalia.

Molokai says it is difficult for him to fit in here. His attitude and perspective is very different from those outside of the Somali community. He still has feelings of anxiety even though he has been removed from his homeland for quite some time. In Canada, he feels physically safe but has difficulty fitting in. Here in Canada, you can argue, you can discuss, and debate. There is no need to be afraid of such things. There is no need to wonder if water will flow from the taps or if a drought will eradicate the crops. It is peaceful and secure yet he still feels uneasy and restless. At least in Somalia, he was accepted for what he was, not viewed with suspicion or disbelief by others. Despite these unsettling feelings, Molokai knows that for him to be successful and help his family, he needs to do well in school, go on to study at College or University, then get a decent job. Here, he can dream of a career. Here, he knows there is a future. In Somalia, the future was dark and forbidding. No one knew what would happen from day to day. But still there are many barriers.

Step One: Teacher-directed Discussions

Have each member of your class read the case study above, the story of Molokai. Divide the class into small groups so they can discuss this. Can they relate to his ill feelings and sense of alienation? Have the class consider a number of issues. What can Molokai do to help himself feel part of the community at large more? Alternatively, what can others do to help him feel accepted, to help ease the unsettling feelings that he still carries within him. There may be those in the class who have emigrated recently or whose parents emigrated from another country. How did they cope with a new country, new values and different perspectives? Do they have any suggestions as to strategies that someone like Molokai might employ to help him feel better about his situation? Have students consider the following scenarios:

- Molokai goes to buy a chocolate bar from a variety store. The store owner eyes him suspiciously. Molokai feels like a criminal even though he hasn't done anything wrong.
- Molokai routinely burns garbage in the back parking lot of his apartment building. When a neighbour objects because the smoke is blowing on to his balcony and it smells bad, Molokai states that he is doing no harm, merely getting rid of unwanted waste.

- Molokai gets into an argument with a classmate. Instead of listening to his point of view, the classmate shoves him to the ground and the "debate" has to be broken up by a hall monitor. Molokai and the classmate both end up in the principal's office and receive a suspension for fighting.

Step Two

Keep the same small discussion groups. Have each group select one of the scenarios and devise some solutions to Molokai's dilemma. The group will then present an oral report to the rest of the class. Make a list of the solutions and strategies on the board for everyone to read. Now introduce the concept of respect into the discussion. Do the student responses involve this idea? That is, is it reasonable to expect Molokai to have respect for the law if he feels like a criminal even though he's done nothing wrong? That if he had respect for his neighbour and for the environment, he wouldn't burn garbage behind his apartment? That if both Molokai and his classmate had respect for each other's point of view, the discussion wouldn't have ended up as a shoving match that got them both into trouble? Have students consider inserting some respect into each of the scenarios at the beginning. What difference would it have made?

Extension Activities

Students will complete at least one of the following:

1. The way in which people interact is represented in their use of language. Language reveals perspective and attitude. Students will take the following terms and phrases and use them in a written context that illustrates how they can be used to demonstrate either respect or disrespect: A separate short paragraph must be written using three of the following words or phrases.

Terms/Phrases: contempt, hatred, trust, violation, admiration, name-calling, discriminate, using your own judgement, blazing a trail, taking pride in, resolution, protest against, out of control, narrow-minded, misunderstanding and coming to terms.

The three completed paragraphs will be handed in for evaluation by the teacher.

2. Divide students into pairs or threes and have them consider these scenarios:
   - A young black man is stopped by the police and questioned for no apparent reason while walking down the street
   - Two girls who are friends are talking and one tells the other she is being sexually harassed by her boss at her part-time job
   - A land developer wants to build a new subdivision on a fragile wetlands
   - A youth without a valid driver's license goes home after school and takes the keys to his mother's car then takes the car out on the road to impress his friends

You are a futurist who makes predictions based on known factors. Select one of the above scenarios and write a detailed description (half page minimum), of what takes place with the statements above as the starting point. What happens next and how does the situation end?

Since you are a futurist and have some measure of control over what happens or does not happen in any given scenario, try writing about it from a different perspective. Inject some mutual respect into the scenario (mutual being between the characters you have created), and then write out the scene as fully and with as much detail as possible. Include some dialogue to make it even more realistic (half page minimum).

Both essays must be handed into the teacher.

3. Divide the students into teams. Have each team member read his/her scenarios to the others in the group. Each group should discuss what they liked/disliked about each member's scenarios. Remember, there is a before and after scenario for each situation and each must be read. Have the group then select one set of scenarios written by a member of the group. That member will then direct the others to "act out" or at least "read out" the two scenarios that have been selected by the group members. These performances will be presented to the rest of the class. If feasible, record the presentations on a mobile device, tablet, digital camera and play them to the class.

4. Keep the same groups as in the previous exercise. For a period of a week, each person in the group will look through the newspaper and cut out articles and stories or print articles from the newspaper's website, that document a situation that demonstrates mutual respect between individuals, organizations or even cultures and are relevant to the law, the environment and/or each other. The group members will also cut or print out articles and stories that depict the other side, i.e., lack of respect between the same. These might consist of crimes committed, traffic violations, disagreements between individuals, groups or organizations, focus on environmental issues or challenges, or racial/cultural discrimination or bias.

The team members will review each of the articles that have been brought in and select one example of a story that illustrates respect and one that does the same for the other side. The group will then recreate each of the stories as if it were a live newscast that was being seen for the first time. The sequence of the presentation of each story (respect vs. disrespect) is to be decided by the group. The team will "rehearse" each story as if it were a short play and then make presentations to the class.

ASSESSMENT AND EVALUATION

Evaluate the class teams on their oral reports from the Discussion section.

Suggested criteria:
- Content (Was the content/strategy clearly articulated and well thought out? Were the points the team made persuasive?)
- Presentation (Was the presentation well-delivered, easy to hear, understand, good vocal quality, gestures, posture etc.?
- Effectiveness (Were the points presented effective, how practical were the suggestions?)
- Teamwork (Did the group work well and effectively together?)

Assess students on their written work from the Activities section.

Suggested criteria:
- Grammatically correct with sentences properly structured, i.e., use of complex sentence structure and correct verb tenses, spelling and punctuation
- Comprehension of the word/phrases—sentences clearly reveal the meaning
- Ideas are expressed clearly
- Information is well-organized

Evaluate students on their presentation work from the Activities section.

Suggested criteria:
- Present information clearly
- What have they done to enhance the presentation?
- Effective use of oral and visual communication

Student self-assessment of teamwork in the Activities section.

Suggested criteria:
- Contribution to group knowledge
- Preparation undertaken for research and investigation
- Articulating goals, devising alternate solutions and selecting best alternatives
- Setting personal goals for working effectively with others

LESSON TWO: FREEDOM

KEY CONCEPTS AND ISSUES

This lesson plan explores the idea of freedom inherent in being a citizen of Canada as compared to elsewhere, the rights and responsibilities that come with citizenship and whether we, as Canadians, take those rights for granted.

OBJECTIVES/OUTCOMES

Students will learn:
- What rights and responsibilities come with Canadian citizenship
- How other systems of government treat their citizens
- To understand what constitutes a moral choice when exercising the rights of citizenship
- How to exercise citizenship rights granted in Canada
- To critically assess situations and seek solutions to real-world challenges
- To work effectively as part of a team

CASE STUDY

Profile of an Activist

Ajay first came to public attention as a result of a series of anti-globalization protests in Toronto 2010. He was once arrested near the campus of the University of Toronto—a "takedown" that was captured on videotape.

But Ajay's development as a political activist began much earlier, going back to at least his high school days in Ontario.

Born to a Hindu father and Catholic mother, Ajay grew up in Scarborough, the east end of the city. His father was an engineer and his mother stayed at home to look after Ajay and his younger brother and sister. Ajay was clearly precocious, inquisitive and very bright: He scored top grades in public school before attending the University of Toronto on a scholarship.

But Ajay says his political awakening began in high school, where he was especially touched by the anti-apartheid struggle in South Africa. Other issues such as homelessness, poverty, racism and corporate power also drew his attention.

It was at university that he began to organize political rallies. Ajay became an on-campus leader for the anti-globalization, anti-racism, anti-poverty student political movement. He could often be seen handing out leaflets, speaking at the students' union, exhorting students to get involved while they rushed from class to class. He led protest marches both on and off campus. He began to generate media attention and was frequently interviewed for the news. Ajay became a recognizable spokesperson for the student protest movement.

After graduation, Ajay stayed on to complete a Master's degree in political science. His protest activities didn't abate, however, but increased in frequency and commitment. Ajay also found he had a talent for organization and uniting different types of groups such as those who were concerned with poverty and homelessness and those whose main cause involved environmental issues.

Ajay's activities brought both success and notoriety. As a result of his now elevated profile and the number of media interviews he'd conducted, he became a target for the authorities. Whenever a large protest was to take place and one where it was clear Ajay was involved, he would be detained by the authorities and held so he was not able to take part. Naturally, these proceedings encouraged him even more and hardened his resolve to continue. In the media, he expressed a sense of outrage at this sort of treatment in a country like Canada that adheres to strict democratic principles. During one such episode, he was held for over a week.

During his protest acts, Ajay was always very careful to stay within the law. He does not condone violence or commit illegal acts. Despite, this, over the next few years, he was arrested several times mainly, his supporters say, because of his visibility. Although he had been charged with various offenses each time, the charges have inevitably been dropped or dismissed quietly after the fact. Some of the protests where Ajay has been involved have gotten out of hand and one in particular got out of hand where the protesters faced riot police and tear gas. A number of people were hurt and more were arrested.

Despite his high profile and treatment by authorities, Ajay seems undeterred and even more determined to speak out on topics and issues that he feels are important. He says he is exercising his democratic rights in a free society to question the status quo and make his views known even if they run counter to mainstream thinking. That is what makes living in a country like Canada, worthwhile, he says, I can do and say what I want and express my opinions, radical or not and I should be able to do this without fear of reprisal.

Step One: Teacher-directed Discussion

Make sure each of your students reads the above profile of Ajay. Divide the class into small groups. Direct them to have a general discussion around the topic of rights and freedoms in a democratic society like Canada. Do your students think Ajay was fairly treated? If so, have them state their reasons why. If not, also have them state their reasons why. Refer back to the listing of the rights of citizenship in the first section of this resource, i.e., Political rights and Legal rights in particular. Make sure these concepts have been introduced into the discussion.

Step Two

Ajay is a member of an organization that is against the globalization of the world (i.e., large commercial conglomerates or brands dominating local markets in many countries). Ask students what they think globalization means and list the challenges that globalization might create. Why would someone like Ajay be against it?

- Have students work individually or in teams and research the concept of globalization. What is it? Why are some individuals and organizations dead set against it? Students should submit a short report on this topic. Maximum length: 1 page.
- Ajay believes in anarchism. What is "anarchism?" Write a short explanation and use the term using three different examples.
- Have students define the term "civil disobedience." Have them give some examples of "civil disobedience." Where does "civil disobedience" fit under or within the rights of citizenship in Canada? Or does it fit? Students will write a short essay on this topic of "civil disobedience" and the rights of citizenship. Minimum length: 1/2 page.

EXTENSION ACTIVITIES

Students will complete at least one of the following:

- In teams or individually, students will prepare a timeline of civil disobedience or dissent in Canada. This may or may not relate to the anti-globalization movement specifically or cast back to an earlier time and incorporate the history of the labour and suffrage movements earlier in the 20th Century. A detailed explanation must accompany the timeline (see _www.cbc.ca/archives/categories/politics/rights-freedoms/voting-in-canada-how-a-privilege-became-a-right/topic---voting-in-canada-how-a-privilege-became-a-right.html_)
- Following is a list of countries, some of which are listed on the Amnesty International Website: _www.amnesty.org_. Students will select one and research the rights (or lack of rights) accorded citizens of that country. They will prepare a detailed report and then compare the "rights" of those citizens in the country selected to those of citizens in Canada. What conclusions might they draw? The countries to choose from are as follows: China, Iran, Saudi Arabia, Iraq, Colombia, Mexico, North Korea, Macedonia, Syria, Guyana, Nigeria, Ivory Coast, the Philippines, Cambodia or Pakistan. Minimum length: 1 page.
- In the aftermath of the terrorist attacks on September 11, 2001, many countries became more security conscious. Canada was no exception. As in other countries like the United States and Britain, Canada introduced new anti-terror legislation in the form of Bill C-36. The Bill adds a definition of "terrorist activity" to the

criminal code and defines an action that is, "taken or threatened for political, religious or ideological purposes and threatens the public or national security by killing, seriously harming or endangering a person, causing substantial property damage that is likely to seriously harm people, or in interfering with or disruption in an essential service, facility or system."

This Bill gives the police the power to:

- Detain a suspected terrorist for 72 hours without charge
- Compel Canadians to testify during an investigation
- Intercept a wider range of private conversations for a longer period of time

Critics have called Bill C-36 draconian and a threat to civil liberties. Some insist that privacy rights will be violated and that Bill C-36 might even override the Canadian Charter of Rights and Freedoms.

Form students into productive teams where they will debate the pros and cons of Bill C-36. The question they will consider is as follows: **Be it resolved that anti-terror legislation is necessary to ensure the security of Canadian citizens and that individual rights may be suppressed for the greater protection of society at large.** Form the teams into the Pro and Con sides. Have each team work together and research the questions and issues and prepare their debating strategies. Stage the debates and have the rest of the class judge the debate and determine which team presented the most compelling case.

For more information, go to *www.cbc.ca/news2/background/cdnsecurity* and do a quick search on Bill C-36.

- Writing for Meaning—the intent of this activity is to enable students to write forcefully and evocatively about an experience that relates specifically to the giving or restricting of freedom based on information, stories and scenarios they uncover through research. For this particular activity, have students consider the case of Nigerian poet and political activist Ken Saro-Wiwa who was subsequently executed for his political activities in that country. Have students research the story of Mr. Saro-Wiwa, the conditions that led to his imprisonment and execution. Students will then write a journal from Mr. Saro-Wiwa's perspective as he waits in prison for the inevitable to happen. The journal entries must be as realistic and credible as possible, evoking feelings and thoughts as well as observations. Have students write in their "journals" for a period of 1week with daily additions to the text. One short paragraph per entry is the minimum required.

ASSESSMENT AND EVALUATION

Evaluate students on their reports and written work from the Discussion and Activities sections.

Suggested criteria:
- Report on globalization (Was the content clearly articulated and well thought out? Were the points the persuasive?)
- Grammatically correct with sentences properly structured, i.e., use of complex sentence structure and correct verb tenses, spelling and punctuation
- Comprehension of the word/phrases—sentences clearly reveal the meaning
- Ideas are expressed clearly
- Information is well-organized

Evaluate students on their oral presentation work from the Activities section.

Suggested criteria:
- Present information clearly
- What have they done to enhance the presentation?
- Effective use of oral and visual communication

Student self-assessment of teamwork in the Activities section.

Suggested criteria:
- Contribution to group knowledge
- Preparation undertaken for research and investigation
- Articulating goals, devising alternate solutions and selecting best alternatives
- Setting personal goals for working effectively with others

LESSON THREE: BELONGING

KEY CONCEPTS AND ISSUES

This lesson explores the idea of belonging and acceptance. How do new Canadians feel that sense or how do they achieve it? Among youth, what is the impact of peer pressure and its effect on being and feeling accepted?

OBJECTIVES/OUTCOMES

Students will learn:
- To make connections to their past
- What the concept of community means
- What it feels like not to belong
- To see the connection between themselves and the community
- How to critically assess information and seek solutions to real-world problems
- How to work collectively in teams

CASE STUDY

Nadia and her family emigrated from Vladivostock, Russia when she was 14 years old. She came with her mother, father and her younger brother, Sergei, who was 8 years old. Although she studied a little bit of English in school back in Russia, Nadia discovered that what she learned there was not of much use here. Despite this fact, Nadia found that when she went to school, her academic standing was still quite good and she qualified for the first year of high school coupled with some intensive English as a Second Language training. Nadia felt she didn't fit in very well. Her English was poor and she couldn't understand the behaviour of her schoolmates. In fact, Nadia had to rely on other Russian girls who had been in Canada for some time and who spoke Russian and English, to help her out and guide her in this new life, to show her the ropes. Her little brother seemed to adapt easily to life in Canada and made friends right away. He picked up English quickly and was good at sports. Nadia's parents, like many of the older generation who emigrate, found it the most difficult to adjust. Nadia's father was a civil engineer in Russia and had to settle for work as a truck driver in Canada. Nadia's mother was an accountant and ended up working as a secretary for a Russian language newspaper publisher. Money has been very tight but at least the family has been self-supporting. Nadia works hard and learns English by talking with her friends, reading as much as she can and watching television. Academically, she struggles at first, then gradually does better. The family lives in a Russian neighbourhood where, if they wanted, English would never be heard nor would they be required to converse in it. Nadia does not have any Canadian friends yet. At present, she only feels comfortable with those who emigrated from Russia, or at least speak Russian. Nadia is a serious girl who appears humourless and doesn't have the carefree demeanour of some of her schoolmates. She thinks that although Canada is much safer than Russia and there are many freedoms here, it is too focused on money and making money and that things are very expensive. She understands and sees how economic class and the emphasis on material goods can divide people. In Russia, everyone struggled because the economy was practically non-existent, or at least experiencing severe upheaval.

Step One : Teacher-Directed Discussion

Have students read Nadia's story. What do they think of her situation? Can any of them relate to what she had experienced? Do class members think that these situations affect boys and girls differently? (Nadia's brother isn't as troubled by the adjustment to a new home.) Is it easier or harder for girls and if so, why do they think this? Or is it just different? Again, have students articulate the possible differences.

Step Two

Suggested Discussion Activities

- Structure a Story—have students write a story about their own immigration experiences whether it relates to them, their parents, grandparents or another relative. Students must relate what "they" knew about Canada, their impressions of the country before they emigrated. They should talk about how they emigrated and the process involved in coming to this country and any incidents, adventures or challenges along the way. Maximum length: 1 page.
- School as Community—Schools are a microcosm of our society and when one is in that environment, it can be taken for granted and accepted without giving it much conscious thought. Divide the class into teams. Each team will make up a demographic survey consisting of questions that are designed to define the school community. Each of the teams will then spread out into the school community and capture the data required either face-to-face through interviews or have students fill out questionnaires. Students may wish to survey lifestyle preferences too, such as: favourite foods, music, leisure activities, etc. The team must write an analysis and report of its findings and present them to the class.

(See *www.accesscable.net/~infopoll/tips.htm* for some good tips on writing useful survey questions.)

Sample categories for the survey:

- Name (optional)
- Date of birth/Age
- Country of origin
- First Language
- Other languages spoken
- Favourite foods
- Musical preferences
- Last movie seen
- Last book read for fun
- Cultural heritage

EXTENSION ACTIVITIES

Students will complete at least one of the following:

- The Belonging Wall—This is an opportunity for students to make a personal statement about themselves in a visual way. On a regular-sized sheet of paper (8.5-in. x 11-in.), students will create a collage that they feel is representative of their values, ideas, attitudes and personalities. What they put on the collage is entirely open-ended (pictures from magazines, the newspaper, downloads from websites). Accompanying their collage will be a detailed explanation that describes the images chosen and how they represent the creator's personality. Once the personal collage is completed, it should be put up on the wall with the others from the class to create "The Belonging Wall." The explanations should be made available to other class members for them to share that information if they wish. Class members may also move pieces of the collage around under the guidance of the teacher, to form different versions of "The Belonging Wall." It should be both interesting and fun to see what comes out of the potential artistic interpretations of the wall-sized collage.
- Response Groups—Divide students into small discussion groups and have them consider the following scenarios:
  - A group of girls won't let one of their classmates into their social circle because they don't think she's cool
  - A young person thinks she is denied a part-time job because of her race
  - Parents won't let their daughter stay out as late as her friends on weekends
  - A young man is pressured into joining a gang because he thinks they accept him as he is
  - A student is asked to let some of his classmates cheat off his test paper

Student groups must select one of the scenarios and discuss the situation and analyze the attitudes and intentions on both sides. They must determine how the situation could be broached and develop strategies that will lead to a resolution of the predicament. Each group must then document their discussion, the analysis and the resolution, then present the same to the class in an oral presentation.

- Connect to Family—Creating a sense of belonging is rooted in the past and how it relates to the present. It is important for anyone to know from where they have come, to take the time to understand family history. Genealogy is a fascinating field of study. There are organizations that have compiled information from municipalities which involves collecting historical information, reviewing death certificates and combing graveyards around the world. This information is then compiled into vast databases of family histories. The Mormon Church is one of the largest holders of genealogical information in the world. Students will then research their family history. There are a number of useful websites that can help get them started. Sometimes, it's a matter of sourcing family photographs and letters, talking to family members particularly those of older generations. Parents may also have compiled a family history for a school project of their own or someone in the family may have done the same. For more recent immigrants, it may be more difficult in some cases. Have students chart or map their family trees so the history is represented visually. A detailed description of the family history must accompany the visual presentation. Some families may have crests, medallions and/or coats of arms and these should be represented too. For teachers, it would be interesting to see how many of the families that emigrated came through the famous Pier 21 in Halifax (_www.pier21.ca_). Another useful website that can help get students started is: _www.collectionscanada.gc.ca_ (National Archives of Canada).

- In or Out—Divide the class in half. Instruct one-half of the class to take a small sheet of paper and write the word "HIP" on it. The other half of the class will do the same except they will write the word "HOP" on their square of paper. The intent of this activity is to get students to experience what it is like to be part of a group that is excluded from the mainstream, subject to privation and no privileges. To begin, the "HIP" group will be the favoured ones, the elite. This might mean letting them out of doing homework for a period, distributing treats or snacks to them only. The "HOP" group is to be treated more harshly. They will stand during the class, will not be permitted to talk, will be spoken to more gruffly for the first half of the class. Teachers may think up other "punishments" as well. In the second half of the class, reverse the roles and now the "HOP" group is in and favoured while the "HIP" group experiences loss of privileges, ones they may have taken for granted. It is up to the teacher to determine how much time may be required to complete the exercise. It may be possible to do within a single period or stretched over two periods, for example. After each group has had its turn, have students write down their impressions. How did they feel when they were part of the "Out" group? Then, compare that to the feeling of being part of the "In" group. They must also document what was learned through this activity and how the experience can be applied to their own relationships and interactions with their peers. Minimum length: 1 page.

ASSESSMENT AND EVALUATION

Evaluate students on their reports and written work from the Discussion and Activities sections.

Suggested criteria:
- Structure a Story, Diary/Logs, School as Community, In or Out, Belonging Wall Report (Was the content clearly articulated and well thought out? Were the points persuasive?)
- Grammatically correct with sentences properly structured, i.e., use of complex sentence structure and correct verb tenses, spelling and punctuation
- Comprehension of the word/phrases—sentences clearly reveal the meaning
- Ideas are expressed clearly
- Information is well-organized

Evaluate students on their oral presentation work from the Activities section.

Suggested criteria:
- Present information clearly
- What have they done to enhance the presentation
- Effective use of oral and visual communication

Evaluate students on their visual presentation work from the Activities section.

Suggested criteria:
- Visually appealing
- Good use of materials
- Well thought out
- Clearly represents the subject

Student self-assessment of teamwork in the Discussion and Activities sections.

Suggested criteria:
- Contribution to group knowledge
- Preparation undertaken for research and investigation
- Articulating goals, devising alternate solutions and selecting best alternatives
- Setting personal goals for working effectively with others

LESSON FOUR: PEACE

KEY CONCEPTS AND ISSUES

This lesson explores the idea of peace and how to achieve it, points to conflict resolution strategies and implementation, and focuses on sources of conflict and how to avoid them.

OBJECTIVES/OUTCOMES

Students will learn:
- To identify potential sources of conflict
- How to defuse situations where conflict arises
- To understand Canada's role as a peacekeeping nation
- To comprehend the impact of Canada's multicultural policies
- How to critically assess information and seek solutions to real-world problems
- How to work collectively in teams

CASE STUDY

Samir and Ruth are high school students who met in Canada. They were attracted to each other and are now a couple. They both came from the Middle East. Samir is a Palestinian and Ruth is Israeli. Although neither is particularly religious, they cannot escape their origins. One thing they have in common is knowledge and experience of conflict. Ruth's family lived outside Tel Aviv. Her parents were originally from Canada who had emigrated to Israel shortly after they got married. The family lived in Israel for almost 20 years. Ruth's father was a reporter for the Jerusalem Post and her mother was a lawyer. Ruth is an only child. As the political situation worsened and the violence continued to escalate, Ruth's parents became increasingly concerned. Ruth's grandparents wanted the family to return home where it was safe, where bombs weren't thrown in the street and extremists didn't blow themselves up in restaurants and on buses. Although it would mean starting over, Ruth's parents didn't want her to continue to be subjected to ongoing terror and fear where, at any moment, something could happen. War was in the air and appeared imminent. Israel seemed to have many enemies and was treated harshly in the court of world opinion. Finally, after many discussions and much soul-searching, Ruth's parents decided to pull up stakes and relocate back to Canada. It wouldn't be easy, but they felt Ruth would have a much better future in a peaceful and safe nation.

Samir was born in Ramallah where he came from a family of prosperous merchants and farmers. He was the oldest of seven children. His family had been doing business with Israeli buyers going back many generations. They were not friends with the Israelis; it was simply business and allowed the family to carry on with their livelihood. All of this changed with the inauguration of the "intifada," the uprising of the Palestinians against the Israelis. Borders were closed. Supply and trade lines were cut off. In a very short period of time, Samir and his family were reduced to poverty, to eking out a bare living. Over time, they sold everything they could, but the economic situation only got worse not better. The family became both destitute and desperate. The only consolation was that everyone else around them, relatives and friends, faced the same circumstances. Samir saw his parents grow frustrated and despondent, saw them losing hope, their spirits low. As a youngster of eight or nine, Samir would join groups of other boys who played in the streets. They would sneak up and watch the Israeli troops and tanks occupying their territory. Samir too would throw rocks and bottles at the Israeli soldiers and tanks. To him, it was exciting, a thrilling sort of game. But it wasn't a game and Samir has a scar above his right eye to prove it. This came from the ricochet of bullet fragments that splintered after hitting a stone-wall near his head. He was lucky that he wasn't blinded. After this incident and fearing for their son's safety, Samir's parents arranged for him to be sponsored by an uncle who lived in Canada. It was arranged finally and Samir left the Middle East and moved to Canada. He keeps in touch with his family and friends mainly through social media, texting, email, and Skype.

Ruth too has many friends she left behind in Israel. She keeps in touch with them constantly, especially when anything happens that she sees or hears about in the news. She and Samir both know the places all too well, understand the situation and feel the despair and hopelessness of a people caught up in a vortex of violence.

Ruth's family and Samir's family both have mixed feelings about the relationship. In Israel, it would have been impossible for them to get together. In Canada, however, anything is possible. They are removed physically and emotionally from the powder keg of the Middle East. It is difficult for them to deny the past; it often gets in the way. Ruth's parents like Samir and try to keep an open mind. Samir's aunt and uncle, who have lived in Canada a long time, also feel conflicted by the relationship but also don't feel they can put a stop to it. In a way, the relationship between Ruth and Samir gives all of them hope for the future.

Step One: Teacher-Directed Discussion

Have students read the story of Ruth and Samir. What do students think of the relationship? Should the past have any bearing on what happens in the present? Do they think that Ruth and Samir will stay together or that the pressure from the past will be too great to bridge the differences between them? Does their story remind students of any other famous couplings? (Hint: Shakespeare and a famous musical from the early 1960s; Romeo and Juliet and West Side Story.).

Step Two

Suggested Discussion Activities

- Write the Ending—Have students in the class write the ending to Ruth and Samir's story. What do they think will happen to them? How will the relationship affect their respective families? As part of the preparation for the story, they must include a separate character description and analysis of Ruth and Samir that may include physical descriptions, lifestyle choices, likes and dislikes, etc. Have students write the stories and then hand them in. Maximum length: 2 pages.
- The "Fight" List—Students will write out a list of things they get into fights, arguments, and disagreements over. This list may be comprised of things they've experienced with friends, siblings, acquaintances, strangers, and/or parents and relatives. Form students into small groups and have them share their lists with the group members. Each group will condense their list into the most common instances of conflict. Each group will appoint a leader who will read the list out to the other group where they will be noted on the board. From the most common situations on the board, another list or master list will be compiled of the most common sources of conflict as identified by the groups.
- Each group will then select a situation from the final master list. They will devise a strategy or series of strategies for attempting to resolve the problem or conflict. This strategy will be documented. Then they will role-play the conflict in front of the rest of the class and apply the strategy to help effect a resolution to the problem. The rest of the class will give verbal feedback on the problem, the role-play and the strategy. Students should be prepared to discover that not all conflicts will be resolved but only "managed." That too, is part of the learning.

There are many conflict resolution websites. Some of them include:

Justice Institute of B.C., *www.jibc.ca*
Mahatma Gandhi Canadian Foundation for World Peace, *www.gandhifoundation.ca*

EXTENSION ACTIVITIES

Students will complete at least one of the following:

- Peacekeeper Is Our Name—Canada is known as a peacekeeping nation. In fact, the origin of peacekeeping started here in Canada. Students will research Canada's role as a peacekeeper and document three campaigns where Canadian troops have taken part and the outcome of each situation. For example, use an online search engine to find digital archives on peacekeeping. Students will prepare a one-page essay on the subject.

- Who Are We?—Under the stewardship of former Prime Minister Pierre Elliott Trudeau, Canada developed a policy of multiculturalism, which many feel has been a major factor in the successful integration of hundreds of thousands of grateful immigrants. For information and statistics on Canada's demographic make up, please see Statistics Canada's website, *www.statcan.gc.ca*. For information on Canada's policy of multiculturalism, see *www.cic.gc.ca/english/ multiculturalism/citizenship.asp?_ga=1.210565013.1474390940.1398796542*. Once students have researched the policy and understand the basics of it, have them think about someone or a group of people they know personally. Once again, it might be family members, schoolmates, friends or acquaintances, and they must think about them specifically in regard to multiculturalism in this country. What effect has the policy had on them? Many immigrants do see Canada as a welcoming place and in addition to its non-violent society, they will cite multiculturalism as one key ingredient to fitting into the way of life here successfully. Students will write the story of those they know who have benefitted from multiculturalism in some way. Maximum length: 1 page.

• Images of Violence—Is violent behaviour influenced by what youth see in the media? Are these images merely a reflection of what happens in our society and the greater world or do these images encourage more violence? This is a debate that may never be resolved but it is unquestionable that images of violence as seen in the media have some influence, if only on perceptions and attitudes rather than actions. Students will keep a journal for a period of a week and document any and all images of war and conflict they see and hear whether it's in the newspaper, magazines, on the radio, on television, websites, in a video or film. Where possible, clip, download or photocopy as many images as possible and make certain the source is clearly cited. Rather than view these images strictly in a negative light, students will select one or two of the most powerful images they have collected and write about how they can help us get to the root of violence and conflict. How can these images be used to understand why violent incidents occur and ultimately lead to some resolution of the conflict? (See *www.mediasmarts.ca* for information about media literacy.) Maximum length: one page.

• Boys and Girls Together—Patterns of behaviour, and in turn of conflict, can be separated along gender lines. We know that boys tend to be more rough-and-tumble and naturally more aggressive. Statistics tell us that male youth have a higher incidence of physical conflict. That doesn't mean it never happens with girls, but it is predominantly a male phenomenon. Girls however, do exhibit a different pattern and tend to get involved in more emotional and behavioural conflicts than boys. Girls tend less to act out these conflicts in a physical sense. Divide the class into teams where they will discuss this issue among themselves. Ensure there is a good gender mix on each team. Why do they think these different sorts of behaviours take place? Is there a way for boys to resolve problems without resorting to physical aggression or violence? Is it a matter of having more outlets for boys at school? In the community? That is, sports activities where boys can vent or act out any pent-up anger or aggression and learn some discipline at the same time?

What other factors are there that students might perceive? In school? At home? In the community? How can boys make an effort to prevent themselves and/or their friends/family/acquaintances from getting drawn into an incident that could lead to acts of violence? The team will research this issue and come up with a detailed list of recommendations and strategies that can help deal with the issue of male aggression and conflict. Each team will make an oral presentation to the class using any visual aids they can such as video, audio, PowerPoint, overheads, drawings, photographs, even a website to help illustrate their approach to the issue.

ASSESSMENT AND EVALUATION

Evaluate students on their reports and written work from the Discussion and Activities sections.

Suggested criteria:
- Write the Story, Fight List, Peacekeeper Is Our Name, Who Are We?, Images of Violence Reports (Was the content clearly articulated and well thought out? Were the points the persuasive?)
- Grammatically correct with sentences properly structured, i.e., use of complex sentence structure and correct verb tenses, spelling and punctuation
- Comprehension of the word/phrases—sentences clearly reveal the meaning
- Ideas are expressed clearly
- Information is well-organized

Evaluate students on their oral presentation work from the Discussion and Activities sections.

Suggested criteria:
- Present information clearly
- What have they done to enhance the presentation
- Effective use of oral and visual communication

Evaluate students on their visual presentation work from the Activities section.

Suggested criteria:
- Visually appealing
- Good use of materials
- Well thought out
- Clearly represents the subject

Student self-assessment of teamwork in the Discussion and Activities sections

Suggested criteria:
- Contribution to group knowledge
- Preparation undertaken for research and investigation
- Articulating goals, devising alternate solutions and selecting best alternatives
- Setting personal goals for working effectively with others

CULMINATING ACTIVITY: DECLARATION OF CITIZENSHIP

KEY CONCEPT AND ISSUES

As a result of completing the previous four lessons, students should be well equipped to develop their own Declaration of Citizenship, i.e., what the concept of citizenship means to them in the most personal sense and how it is defined in their own terms.

In the introductory section, students were exposed both to the rights and responsibilities of citizenship. They understand clearly there are benefits to becoming a citizen, but it isn't a free ride nor something to be taken lightly.

Begin by explaining to students that they have undergone a process and in doing so, have learned about four key areas that have an impact on their ability to fully and actively participate in Canadian society. Those four key areas are: Respect, Freedom, Belonging and Peace. All of the knowledge and information they have gleaned should now be used to create their own, personal Declaration of Citizenship.

Here are a few suggestions for some preparatory steps:
- Review the Universal Declaration of Human Rights (*www.un.org/en/documents/udhr*)
- Review the Rights of Persons Belonging to National, Ethnic, Religious or Linguistic Minorities which was adopted by the United Nations General Assembly in December 1992 (*www.un-documents.net/a47r135.htm*)
- Talk to family and friends about their perceptions of the rights and responsibilities of Citizenship
- Attend a political event or rally
- Get involved in a cause in which you believe
- Do some volunteer work
- Mentor a younger person or help a peer

Once the Declaration of Citizenship is completed, it should be posted in the class for other classes and the community to view. Turn this into a media event and invite local papers, radio, and television to participate. Invite community leaders and school board officials. Create a Declaration of Citizenship website or social media account and invite others to participate. You may wish to turn this into a public event and have the Declarations made during an assembly or an outdoor gathering, weather permitting. The Declarations can be in any form the student wishes and as colourful and creative as desired. The single most important requirement is the Declaration itself must be thoughtful and sincere.

= LESSON FIVE

THE CANADIAN NORTHERN PROJECT
CANADIAN SOVEREIGNTY IN THE ARCTIC

The concept of sovereignty is an evolving one. It has traditionally focused on the rights of a country to control a territory (the land and its inhabitants) legitimately without interference from other countries. Now, instead of focusing on rights, sovereignty is being considered in terms of responsibilities, especially the responsibility of a country to protect, and have authority over, its territory and to be perceived as protecting it and having authority over it. Sovereignty is also thought to include stewardship over the territory.

GRADE LEVEL:
9 – 12

CURRICULA THEMES:

Social Studies,
World History,
World Geography

LESSON ONE: MULTICULTURALISM AND CANADA'S NORTH

GRADE LEVEL:

Grades 9-12

DURATION:

Five to Eight classroom periods

CURRICULUM LINKS:

Social Studies
World History
World Geography
(For specific curriculum links, please visit *www.teachmag.com/cnp*)

The goal is for students to reflect on their understanding of multiculturalism and learn how it connects to Canada's North, including Canada's sovereignty in the North.

Students will explore the role of the Inuit and Aboriginal peoples as stewards of Canada's North and share ways to support and enhance this role. By participating in this activity, students will research to learn more about the culture of these fellow Canadians. They will gain a better understanding of how they have been the traditional stewards of Canada's North, and reflect on whether they may be best equipped to continue as the stewards of Canada's North.

They will read the chapter in the graphic novel, *Project North: Canadian Sovereignty in the Arctic*, that describes what Alex and ZaZi learn about multiculturalism and Canada's role in the North as they do their school project.

MATERIALS REQUIRED

- Computers, tablets, or mobile devices with Internet access
- Detailed map of Canada's North:
  http://maps.nationalgeographic.com/maps/atlas/north-america-geophysical.html
- Writing paper and tools or note-taking programs and apps
- Graphic novel *Project North: Canadian Sovereignty in the Arctic* available to download for free at *www.teachmag.com/cnp*

LEARNING OUTCOMES

Students will:
- Increase their knowledge of Canadian history and geography
- Analyze major issues involving the rights, responsibilities, roles, and status of individual citizens and groups in a local, national, and global context
- Explain, analyze, and compare the effectiveness of various methods of influencing public policy
- Explore the concept of protecting Canadian identity and sovereignty
- Examine one or more aspects of multiculturalism in the Canadian context

BACKGROUND

The concept of sovereignty is an evolving one. It has traditionally focused on the rights of a country to control a territory (the land and its inhabitants) legitimately without interference from other countries. Now, instead of focusing on rights, sovereignty is being considered in terms of responsibilities, especially the responsibility of a country to protect, and have authority over, its territory and to be perceived as protecting it and having authority over it. Sovereignty is also thought to include stewardship over the territory.

For thousands of years, Canada's North has been home to Inuit and Aboriginal peoples. Their unique culture, one of many within Canada, is a reflection of their northern environment and their close relationship with the land.

"The concept of the land included not just the earth itself, but all of nature: plants, animals, water, ice, wind and sky. Nature and Inuit are one. They have depended on each other for centuries and any change or alteration to just one aspect can unbalance the whole."
– Innuuqatigitt curriculum, page 31

While climate change in the North is affecting the way of life for the Inuit people in a detrimental way, it is also drawing international attention to the North as a possible Northwest passage is emerging. Thus, what is detrimental to the culture and even survival of the Inuit may be of economic benefit to others.

Step One: Teacher-Led Discussion

Begin with a general discussion about multiculturalism and what it means. Explain that Canada has an official policy of multiculturalism. It was announced in 1971 and acknowledged the diversity within the country; it encouraged cultural pluralism, instead of assimilation. It suggested the Canadian identity was based on an acceptance of ethnic difference. In 1982, multiculturalism was mentioned in section 27 of the Canadian Charter of Rights and Freedoms.[1] It states: "This Charter shall be interpreted in a manner consistent with the preservation and enhancement of the multicultural heritage of Canadians."

Remind students that Canada is a land of immigrants, and that people have been coming to live in Canada for hundreds of years. Draw their attention to a map of Canada and indicate the Arctic regions. Ask the students, who were the first inhabitants of this land? Discuss the word Inuit, and tell students it means "the people." Ask them to share anything they already know about the Inuit, their culture, their daily lives, their traditional system of governance, and their contemporary way of life.

Step Two

Tell students that Canada's North, ancestral home of the Inuit, has become an area of interest to many countries. They are eyeing its natural resources (uranium, natural gas, and diamonds) with interest and, as global warming is causing the northern ice to melt, these other countries are becoming interested in the possibility of a Northwest passage through the area. They are challenging whether this land and its people, are actually within Canada's political sphere. (The students will learn more about this in Lesson Two.) Explain that the four lessons in this program will be investigating different aspects of this issue.

---

1 *www.parl.gc.ca/information/library/PRBpubs/936-e.htm*

Also, explain to students that, throughout these four lessons, they will be reading a graphic novel *Project North: Canadian Sovereignty in the Arctic*. It follows the progress of Alex and ZaZi as they do their school project on sovereignty in the North. It introduces the major themes and issues about Canada's sovereignty in the North. They may read the book at this stage, or they may choose to read it in sections, as they move through the subsequent lessons. Have students summarize one important theme of the graphic novel to a partner. The partner will make notes on the summary to document what the student said. This will be handed in to the teacher.

Step Three

Tell students that the focus of steps three and four of this lesson is on answering these questions:
- Are the Inuit uniquely equipped to be stewards of Canada's North and, if so, why?
- What does this mean to them, and to Canada?
- How does this influence the challenges to Canada's traditional role in the Arctic?
- How can you educate students within your school about the Inuit to help raise their profile as fellow Canadians and enhance their role as stewards of the North?

First, have the students define the word "steward" (one who protects or looks after nature, public property, or money; one who manages another's property or affairs). Have them look for the more recent definition of environmental "stewardship." (Environment Canada defines it as "being the act of entrusting the careful and responsible management of the environment and natural resources for the benefit of the general community."[2]) Discuss reasons why Canada's North needs stewards.

Read to students this excerpt from a speech called "Inuit and the Canadian Arctic: Sovereignty Begins at Home" made by Mary Simon (President of the Inuit Tapiriit Kanatami, which in English means "Inuit are united in Canada").

"The Arctic is in urgent need of attention by all Canadians and, indeed, by the world community. ... As leader of the national Inuit organization, I am determined to generate public interest and galvanize political attention on Arctic issues....

Canada is an "Arctic nation." The Arctic ... is a vital part of our country, and its peoples contribute to the cultural and social diversity that we value so dearly. ...

Together we must build robust and sustainable northern communities. A healthy, confident and prosperous Inuit population will create the foundation for keeping the Arctic firmly within Canada. ...

For us, the Inuit, it is our homeland – our special place on Earth. But for all Canadians, the Arctic must become part of our shared sense of who and what we are,

---

2 EC 2005, www.science-metrix.com/pdf/SM_2004_016_EC_Report_Stewarship_Nanotechnology_Environment.pdf

of what defines us, and what we are accountable for – not just a remote region with beautiful icescapes and polar bears.

Part of that accountability is accepting that the Arctic is a place where people live, where families are raised, where problems need solving, and where resources exist that will continue to nurture human development, and help finance this wonderful place called Canada."

Discuss Mary Simon's comments, for example:
- Why might some people have difficulty accepting that the Arctic is a place where people live?
- What does she mean by "accountability?"
- Why do you think she mentions resources as a source of financing for the country?
- Why do you think her speech is called "Sovereignty Begins at Home?"

Think about Simon's biases and why she might hold these views. For example, how might it benefit her and the Inuit to generate public interest? Also, consider whether you think all Inuit share her views.

Now remind the students that the land has special meaning to the Inuit. They are connected to the land. It sustains them, and they feel a responsibility to care for it. Scientists believe climate change will be more pronounced in high latitudes.[3] The change in temperatures is causing changes in the natural environment, for example, there is a longer sea-ice free season, there are more insects, more pronounced windstorms, and shorter snowmobile seasons over sea-ice.[4]

Read this quote from Sheila Watt-Cloutier, former chair of the Inuit Circumpolar Conference (Canada), speaking in Ottawa, in 2002:

"Inuit are not prepared to be seen, to be treated, or to act as powerless victims of external forces over which we have no control. In fact, Inuit are involved in every aspect of life that affects us, from the science to the policy, in the communities, in Canada, in the circumpolar Arctic, and globally. Unfortunately, the federal government seems to think our role is to adapt to climate change. But that is only part of our role. We intend to bring our concerns, interests, and perspectives, and those of the Arctic more broadly, to the attention of international decision-makers. We must give climate change in the Arctic a human face -- an Inuk face -- and we must show climate change negotiators that impacts in the Arctic foreshadow impacts around the globe. We want to do this in co-operation with the Government of Canada and other Arctic states."

---

[3] *www.inuitcircumpolar.com/icc-reports.html*
[4] *www.inuitcircumpolar.com/icc-reports.html*

With the students, discuss these questions:
- Are the Inuit particularly vulnerable to climate change, as a people, compared to other Canadians?
- How does climate change threaten the survival of the Inuit as a people?
- How does this connect to the role of the Inuit as stewards of the North?

Lastly, explain to them that one theory of sovereignty states that demonstrating use of the North gives legitimacy to a country's claim to the region. Read them the following quote:

"The Inuit have been using the Arctic for thousands of years. It's their historic use and occupancy of the sea-ice that provides the basis for Canada's claim in the Northwest Passage. It's they who have given us all that they have, in pursuit of a quintessentially Canadian dream."

– Michael Byers and Jack Layton,
in "How to Strengthen Our Arctic Sovereignty" in The Tyee, Sept 2007 [5]

Have the students gather in small groups and tell them they are now going to synthesize the information they have just been exploring as they work to answer these questions:
- Are the Inuit uniquely equipped to be stewards of Canada's North and, if so, why? Has the policy of multiculturalism played a part in this, and if so, how?
- What might it mean for the Inuit themselves to be considered "Canada's stewards of the North?"
- How might demonstrating that the Inuit are Canada's stewards of the North influence the challenges to Canada's claims to Northern lands?

Allow the students time to do individual research, seeking out, in particular, Inuit perspectives on all these questions, and then write responses. Have each group do a brief oral presentation of their answers to the class.

Step Four

Remind the students that the Inuit had no written history until recently; they have a tradition of oral history, passing down stories, information, and wisdom through stories and narrative. Tell them they will create a presentation for students at school that includes an oral element and addresses this final question:

- How can you educate students within your school about the Inuit in order to raise their profile as fellow Canadians and enhance their role as stewards of the North?

Encourage them to brainstorm suggestions, such as hosting an assembly, putting on a play for students, doing presentations in each classroom, and so on.

---

[5] *http://thetyee.ca/Views/2007/09/06/ColdReality/print.html*

With your assistance, have the students discuss and then choose one idea. Give them time to set a goal for themselves, to formalize the idea into a plan, and to create an agenda (or a step-by-step process), for accomplishing the plan and assigning duties. During the discussion, help focus their thinking by asking: "Do you think this will educate students within your school about the Inuit in order to raise their profile as fellow Canadians and enhance their role as stewards of the North?"

Allow students time to research for their presentation. Guide them toward sources that convey a breadth of information of the Inuit past and present, including online newspaper articles, reports of circumpolar summits, and the website of the Inuit Tapiriit Kanatami. Remind them that they will need to educate other students about the concept of stewardship and offer evidence that the Inuit are "stewards of the North." They will need to briefly describe Canada's traditional political role in the North and how it is currently being challenged. Encourage them to relay Inuit points of view, using their own words directly, whenever possible.

Help make arrangements for them to visit other classrooms or host other classrooms in a specified location.

Step Five

When the scheduled day(s) for the presentation arrive(s), provide help as needed for the students.

Step Six

Discuss as a class the results of the presentation. Help the students evaluate the process they created, and establish whether their final goals were met, and how they know these goals were met. Have them think about what they might do differently next time.

OPTIONAL EXTENSION ACTIVITIES

- In her Globe and Mail article, "Fund Inuit, not Canadian, Arctic sovereignty,"[6] author Marie Wadden writes: *"How can Canada claim to "own" the Arctic when it can't provide adequate housing, health care and schooling for our Inuit, who number only in the tens of thousands (about **40 000** in the Arctic) but live in **26** communities stretched out over more than **4000** kilometres, from Nunatsiavut on the Labrador Sea to the Inuvialuit homeland of the western Arctic. Instead of soldiers "guarding" our Arctic borders, we should have Inuit citizens who feel truly a part of this country, who are respected and given the necessary tools to succeed in the 21st century. … Let's stop funding Canadian*

[6] *www.theglobeandmail.com/news/opinions/fund-inuit-not-canadian-arctic-sovereignty/article1256334*

Arctic sovereignty and, instead, fund Inuit Arctic sovereignty. If we're lucky and do the right thing, they may let us call them 'Canadian Inuit.'"

Explain how you think Wadden's view is different than, or similar to, Simon's view. Write a short first-person narrative from the perspective of someone who believes Canada may be trying to take advantage of the Inuit people in order to keep the North.

- There may be people who still believe that all Inuit live in permanent igloos and hunt by dogsled. Have students create a poster showing two contemporary scenes: one of an Inuit family living on the land in a traditional lifestyle, and one of an Inuit family living in the city of Iqaluit in a modern lifestyle. They can add a heading for each scene, captions, and title the poster: Inuit Myth Buster!

- *"I used to be able to predict the weather, but now I often get it wrong."*
  – Akumalik, 73, Arctic Bay, Nunavut, through translator[7]

Pose the question again: In what ways are the two issues—climate change in the North and difference of opinion about Northern sovereignty—connected? Interested students can do further research to learn about climate change in the North, in particular, its effects on the Inuit peoples. Have them look for personal Inuit accounts of changes to the northern ecosystem, as well as evidence as to who is trying to solve this problem and whether the experience and knowledge of the Inuit people is being taken into account.

- Students can research to find all the countries where Inuit traditionally live. Have them mark these locations on a world map. Then have them look up, and read, "A Circumpolar Inuit Declaration on Sovereignty in the Arctic." Have them discuss, in partners, section 1: Inuit and the Arctic. (They will look more closely at the rest of the document in Lesson 2.) Ask them to think about why the Inuit felt it necessary to convene and create these statements.

ASSESSMENT AND EVALUATION RUBRICS

General

Discussion
Level 1   Did not participate or contribute to the teacher-directed discussions
Level 2   Participated somewhat in the teacher-directed discussions
Level 3   Actively participated in the teacher-directed discussions
Level 4   Made a significant contribution to the teacher-directed discussions

---

[7] *www.canada.com/vancouversun/story.html?id=50c89709-aa8f-4da9-bef8-27e051d2cfc8&k=26596*

Content
Level 1   Demonstrated limited understanding of concepts, facts, and terms
Level 2   Demonstrated some understanding of concepts, facts, and terms
Level 3   Demonstrated considerable understanding of concepts, facts, and terms
Level 4   Demonstrated thorough understanding of concepts, facts, and terms

Written Work
Level 1   Written report had many grammatical errors, is poorly structured and confusing
Level 2   Written report was generally clear, but has numerous grammatical errors
Level 3   Written report was well-structured and clear, but has a few significant/grammatical errors
Level 4   Written report was very clear, well-organized with few errors

Oral Presentation
Level 1   Oral report was confusing, lacked emphasis and energy, with no discussion resulting
Level 2   Oral report was adequate, but lacked emphasis and energy, with little discussion resulting
Level 3   Oral report was clear and well presented, but lacked some emphasis and energy with a good discussion resulting
Level 4   Oral report was clear and enthusiastically presented, with energetic discussion resulting

Teamwork
Level 1   1 or 2 members dominated the team, very little cooperation
Level 2   Majority of the group made a contribution, with some recognition of individual strengths but cooperation was superficial
Level 3   Most members made a significant contribution, with a good level of cooperation
Level 4   All members made a significant contribution, individual strengths were recognized and used effectively, excellent co-operation among group members

Specific

Step One
Level 1   Student has a poor understanding of multiculturalism
Level 2   Student has a basic understanding of multiculturalism
Level 3   Student has a good understanding of multiculturalism
Level 4   Student has an exemplary understanding of multiculturalism

Step Two
Level 1   Student poorly communicated a summary to a partner
Level 2   Student adequately communicated a summary to a partner
Level 3   Student communicated a summary to a partner well
Level 4   Student communicated a summary to a partner in an exemplary manner

Step Three
Level 1   Student has a poor understanding of the concept of Inuit stewardship
Level 2   Student has a basic understanding of the concept of Inuit stewardship
Level 3   Student has a good understanding of the concept of Inuit stewardship
Level 4   Student has an exemplary understanding of the concept of Inuit stewardship

Step Four
Level 1   Student exhibited poor participation in the planning of the presentation
Level 2   Student exhibited basic participation in the planning of the presentation
Level 3   Student exhibited good participation in the planning of the presentation
Level 4   Student exhibited exemplary participation in the planning of the presentation

Step Five
Level 1   Student exhibited poor participation in the class presentation
Level 2   Student exhibited basic participation in the class presentation
Level 3   Student exhibited good participation in the class presentation
Level 4   Student exhibited exemplary participation in the class presentation

Step Six
Level 1   Student demonstrated a poor ability to evaluate the presentation
Level 2   Student demonstrated a basic ability to evaluate the presentation
Level 3   Student demonstrated a good ability to evaluate the presentation
Level 4   Student demonstrated an exemplary ability to evaluate the presentation

RESOURCES

Diversity Watch (info about Inuit)
www.diversitywatch.ryerson.ca/backgrounds/inuit.htm

The Curriculum from the Inuit Perspective: Inuuqatigitt curriculum
www.ece.gov.nt.ca/early-childhood-and-school-services/school-services/curriculum-k-12

Land Stewardship Centre
www.landstewardship.org

Mary Simon's speech: "Inuit and the Canadian Arctic: Sovereignty Begins at Home"
www.muse.jhu.edu/login?auth=0&type=summary&url=/journals/journal_of_canadian_studies/v043/43.2.simon.html

Another Mary Simon speech
www.itk.ca/media/speech/sovereignty-begins-home-inuit-and-canadian-arctic

A Circumpolar Inuit Declaration on Sovereignty in the Arctic
www.itk.ca/front-page-story/circumpolar-inuit-declaration-arctic-sovereignty

Inuit Tapiriit Kanatami
www.itk.ca

Unikkaaqatigiit: Putting the Human Face on Climate Change—Perspectives from Inuit in Canada
www.itk.ca/publication/unikkaaqatigiit-perspectives-inuit-canada

LESSON TWO: GOVERNANCE AND CANADA'S NORTH

DURATION:

Five to Eight classroom periods

CURRICULUM LINKS:

Social Studies
World History
World Geography
(For specific curriculum links, please visit *www.teachmag.com/curricula*)

Students will draw on the information they learned in Lesson One about the Inuit and their stewardship of Canada's North, and learn more about the struggle for sovereignty in the North (for example, why it is of such interest currently). They will be introduced to the goals, challenges, and limitations of international law. They will explore the concept of sovereignty as an evolving one and the implications of this as countries vie to stake their claim to territory in the Arctic, the "last frontier." The project engages students in learning more about the structures currently in place to establish governance of the Arctic, assessing Canada's current activities there, and then working together on a project to evaluate and assess the international structure set up to manage these disputes and suggest alternative rules of governance.

They will read further in the graphic novel, *Project North: Canadian Sovereignty in the Arctic* to learn more about governance and its connection to Canada's sovereignty in the North.

KEY CONCEPTS AND ISSUES

Students will explore the concept of governance and how it connects to issues related to Canada's North.

MATERIALS REQUIRED

- Computers, tablets, or mobile devices with Internet access
- Detailed map of Canada's North:
  http://maps.nationalgeographic.com/maps/atlas/north-merica-geophysical.html
- Writing paper and tools or computers and mobile devices with word processing or note-taking apps
- Graphic novel *Project North: Canadian Sovereignty in the Arctic* available to download for free at *www.teachmag.com/cnp*

EXPECTATIONS/OUTCOMES

Students will:
- Demonstrate an understanding of Canada's political, social, and economic systems in a global context
- Recognize the purpose of laws within the Canadian, and international context
- Demonstrate an understanding of an international issue affecting Canada
- Recognize the achievements of Aboriginal organizations (e.g., Inuit Tapiriit Kanatami) in gaining recognition of the rights of Aboriginal peoples in Canada

- Recognize possible differences in perspectives on issues of significance to Canadians
- Apply the concepts of stewardship and sustainability to analyze a current national or international issue
- Evaluate the role of government in maintaining sovereignty in the North, and identify possible courses of action necessary for achieving this outcome
- Distinguish between primary and secondary sources of information; evaluate the credibility of sources and information; and organize and record information gathered through research

BACKGROUND

The North is becoming of increasing interest to various countries because global warming is melting ice, opening previously ice-covered waterways in the Arctic region. The result is more accessibility. Many countries are now expressing interest in the region as they recognize its potential for resource exploitation and development, and as a route of passage across the top of North America. Some are claiming sovereignty over portions of the Arctic seabed; many are claiming rights of access through the Northwest Passage.

The country that establishes sovereignty in this region will derive significant benefits. Canada's traditional sovereignty in the North is being challenged by many countries, including the United States, Russia, Iceland, Denmark, Finland, Norway, and Sweden. Canada is asserting that the Northwest Passage represents internal waters; other countries are arguing that these are international waters. Canada has been defending its authority over the North diplomatically, and it has been making promises to increase its presence in the region. Its commitments include building a deep-water port and supplying a fleet of limited range Arctic patrol boats. So far, however, these promises have not been delivered.

There is some general agreement about how to address some of these disputes. Because most of the region at issue is not land, but impermanent ice, it falls under the UN Convention on the Law of the Sea (UNCLOS), a convention ratified by 150 nations. The convention states that nations have the right to control the belt of shoreline along their coasts, which is 12 nautical miles (22.2 km). Some Arctic waterways are as much as 100 kilometres wide, however, due to increased ice loss as a result of climate change. This is providing widening shipping lanes, increasing foreign ship traffic. Some scientists predict the Northwest Passage could be ice-free by 2040. This makes these waters very attractive to commercial shipping interests from Europe and the Far East, as well as cruise shipping. In addition the receding ice removes barriers to exploring for oil, natural gas, diamonds, gold, and iron ore.

Canada is claiming these waters are internal and not open to foreign ships without permission. Other countries are also claiming governance over sections of the seabed (for example, Russia claims sovereignty over the Lomonosov Ridge, a huge undersea mountain chain that stretches across the Arctic Ocean from Siberia to Ellesmere Island and Greenland). The UNCLOS requires these disputes be resolved through presenting scientific evidence proving areas claimed are geographically linked to the country, or its Arctic islands. Several, including Canada, are undertaking extensive mapping in order to comply. Ironically, Canadian, Russian, American, and Norwegian scientists are working together to collect the necessary data to further their own interests.

Step One: Teacher-Led Discussion

Begin with a general discussion about governance and what that means. Ask students why there are national laws, and give some examples of these. Ask them why there are international laws (traditionally, to deal with conflict between states). To supplement their discussion, tell them that international laws develop in several ways, for example:[1]

- They arise out of international treaties and agreements between states
- They begin as practices that become customary over time and end up as laws
- They arise out of a commonality of principles in various states that become part of the accepted body of international law
- They are recommended by international legal scholars and accepted by political leaders

Point out that because much of international law is based on practices already followed by states, it is often adhered to; frequently there is no mechanism in place to enforce international laws that are not adhered to. There are some international (or supranational) institutions to help maintain international laws, such as the International Court of Justice, the European Court of Justice, and the International Criminal Court.

There are international laws that deal with economic law (trade and commerce), security law, diplomatic laws, environmental law, the law of war, and human rights law.

Tell students that the Arctic has been called "one of the last global frontiers" and ask what they think that means, specifically, what that might mean for Canada. Have them read further in the graphic novel, and then supplement what they learn there by reviewing with them the following information:

- In a 2007 article in The Epoch Times, Cindy Drukier states: "In terms of land claims, it is an accepted geopolitical fact that the British ceded the 36,500

1 www.beyondintractability.org/essay/international_law/?nid=1019

plus island Arctic Archipelago to Canada in 1880. Our claim to maritime sovereignty, however, is more shaky."[2]

- There are disputes about who has governance over regions in the North. There is a dispute over the Lomonosov Ridge. Russia claims sovereignty over this huge undersea mountain chain that stretches across the Arctic Ocean from Siberia to Ellesmere Island and Greenland. In 2007, they planted a flag on the North Pole seabed to stake their claim.

- Canada also claims this section of the seabed. According to the United Nations Convention on the Law of the Sea (UNCLOS) an area has to be geographically linked to the country, or its Arctic islands, making a claim for it.[3] Canada and Denmark scientists worked together to provide evidence that the Lomonosov Ridge is an extension of the North American continent. Russia has also presented its own study however. Countries submitted more evidence in 2013.

- There are other disputed areas as well:
  - Denmark claimed uninhabited Hans Island and put up a flag there in 2002. Canada disputed this claim and removed the flag.
  - Canada claims the waters of the Arctic Archipelago, including the Northwest Passage, as inland waters. Other countries, including the United States, claim they are not. They claim navigational rights here, allowing them the right of transit passage.
  - Canada and the United States dispute a border in the Beaufort Sea. There are petroleum reserves in the area that would be affected.

Have students read on in the graphic novel *Project North: Canadian Sovereignty in the Arctic*.

Step Two

Tell the students that this part of the lesson will focus on a conversation about the North as both homeland to the Inuit and a region over which Canada wishes to maintain governance. Ask them to reflect on what they learned in Lesson One and suggest whether they can see how these two statements might signify either conflict or common purpose.

Review with the students the current accepted concept of sovereignty as the responsibility of a country to protect, and have authority over, its territory and to be perceived as protecting it and having authority over it. As the students have discussed in Lesson One, sovereignty is also thought to include stewardship over the territory. Have two volunteers then define sovereignty in their own words and record these definitions on the board.

[2] *www.theepochtimes.com/news/7-7-12/57562.html*
[3] *www.canada.com/topics/news/world/story.html?id=b7be4e45-1244-478e-864e-a6150b0bf679*

"Sovereignty is a question of exercising, actively, your responsibilities in an area."
– Former Canadian National Defence Minister Bill Graham[4]

"Canada has a choice when it comes to defending our sovereignty in the Arctic; either we use it or we lose it."
– Prime Minister Stephen Harper, 2007

Read to students the above quotes, and ask them whether they believe Canada has stewardship over the North and is "using" the region. Recall with students what they have learned about the land and culture of the Inuit in Lesson One, and suggest that the issue of governance in the North is of great importance to the Inuit. Mention that Canada often points to the presence of the Inuit in the North as evidence of Canada's "use" of the region. Tell them that the Arctic Archipelago is a vast region, representing 40 per cent of Canada's territory. Remind them that, as noted in the graphic novel, the Arctic Archipelago is policed by the Canadian Rangers, an army reserve unit made up of Inuit who patrol with snowmobiles and rifles, "controlling" the land surrounding the disputed waters. This is known as Operation Nunalivut, Inukitut for "Land that is ours."

Next, tell students you are going to read them excerpts from speeches by two different people (or have a student read the same). Read this first one aloud. (It is from a speech by Mary Simon, former president of the Inuit Tapiriit Kanatami).

"There are three key messages that I would like to give you today....

The first is that the Arctic is a region of Canada whose time has come. Sovereignty, environmental, economic development and social policy factors all support this conclusion.

The second is that Sovereignty begins at home. Canada cannot successfully assert its national agenda in the Arctic while ignoring the state of civil society in the Arctic.

The third is that the key to sustainable Arctic policies and creative policy making in Canada must be anchored in establishing a constructive partnership with Inuit."

After making sure the students understand her points, read the students this excerpt. (It is from a speech made by Prime Minister Stephen Harper in August 2006 in Iqaluit, Nunavut.)

"... [Y]ou can't defend Arctic sovereignty with words alone. It takes a Canadian presence on the ground, in the air and on the sea.... I am here today to make it absolutely clear there is no question about Canada's Arctic border. It extends from the northern tip of Labrador all the way up the East coast of Ellesmere Island to Alert.

---

4 Graeme Smith, "Graham focuses on Arctic during visit to Russia," The Globe and Mail [Toronto], 2 September 2005, p. A5

Then it traces the western perimeter of the Queen Elizabeth Islands down to the Beaufort Sea. From there it hugs the coasts of the Northwest Territories and Yukon to the Canada-U.S. border at Alaska. All along the border, our jurisdiction extends outward 200 miles into the surrounding sea, just as it does along our Atlantic and Pacific coastlines.

No more. And no less....

... [The] government's first obligation is to defend the territorial integrity of its borders. And this will become more important in the decades to come - because northern oil and gas, minerals and other resources of the northern frontier will become ever more valuable. The technologies used in Arctic resource extraction and transport are increasingly sophisticated and affordable. And the Northwest Passage is becoming more accessible every year: Some scientists even predict it will be open to year-round shipping within a decade.

In short, the economics and the strategic value of northern resource development are growing ever more attractive and critical to our nation. And trust me, it is not only Canadians who are noticing. It is no exaggeration to say that the need to assert our sovereignty and take action to protect our territorial integrity in the Arctic has never been more urgent.

The North is poised to take a much bigger role in Canada's economic and social development. It is attracting international attention, investment capital, people, and commercial and industrial development.

Therefore the Government of Canada has an enormous responsibility to ensure that development occurs on our terms.

In particular, we must ensure the unique ecosystem of the North, and the unique cultural traditions of the First Peoples of the North, are respected and protected."

After making sure they understand the points in this speech, ask them to guess who the speakers are, and explain their reasons. After the discussion, tell them the names of the speakers.

Step Three

Have students review the current governance system in place in the North to assess what Canada must do in order to prove its sovereignty in the Arctic. Begin by reviewing the definition of sovereignty and encouraging students to pick out the key points that Canada needs to prove (it is patrolling and protecting the North, establishing a presence in, or "using" the North; other governments must recognize Canada's sovereignty). Have students do some research to learn more about:

- Canada's history in the North
- The promises made by governments about securing the North
- The promises made by governments to the Inuit about their role in the North
- How Canada is currently policing the North (including Radarsat-2)
- How Canada is currently handling decision-making in the North
- The scientific evidence that Canada is preparing to bolster its territorial claims in the North

After the students have had a chance to do research, meet as a class and engage the students in an evaluation of Canada's position and make suggestions about how the country might strengthen its claims to the North while following the existing laws and conventions.

Step Four

Tell the students they will assess the existing structure that is in place to resolve disputes about sovereignty in the "last frontier" and, if they believe it necessary, suggest alternatives to some parts of it or the whole structure.

First, have them do some preliminary research to find out more about other international bodies or international laws. Have them find out what types of behaviour are governed internationally, why, and how the rules or laws are upheld. Suggest that they think about what limitations there are to these laws and courts, but also have them look for examples where these laws are helping prevent, or reduce, conflicts and disputes.

Meet as a group and discuss what they have learned. Now have them reflect on their new project—evaluating the governance system in place in the Arctic and suggesting alternatives—and together, arrive at some key questions that will help them in their analysis, such as:

- What do we already know about how disputes about sovereignty in the North are being resolved? (Examples: UNCLOS is requiring countries to provide scientific proof of geographical links to undersea regions; there is an accepted definition of sovereignty which requires policing, and maintaining a presence in, the North, as well as a common perception that this is being achieved)
- How did this governance system come about? Do all countries accept it? (Example: the United States has not ratified UNCLOS)
- What are advantages of this governance system? (Examples: based on custom and precedent; because there are no written rules about some of the verification methods, this respects the integrity of all countries, forces them to take a big-picture look at the situation, and avoids them becoming entrenched in bickering about minor letter-of-the-law points and minutiae; so far, this governance system seems to be helping countries avoid direct conflict)
- What are possible difficulties with it? (Examples: there is no set-in-stone process for confirming sovereignty, for example, how do countries agree on their

"perceptions" about whether or not another country is maintaining a presence in the North; how do countries which disagree express their grievances?; does it offer a foolproof failsafe method for avoiding conflict as the stakes become higher?)
- Is this the best system of governance for tackling the issues? What elements might you want to change, and why? What alternative form of governance would you set up, and why? What advantages or difficulties might it present?

Step Five

Provide pairs of students with sufficient time to reflect on research they have already done and to conduct any additional research required. Remind them of the importance in using accurate sources. Have them keep track of all the sources they use. Review the difference between primary and secondary sources and their respective values.

(You may wish to refer them to the model negotiation statement prepared in 2008 by two teams of non-governmental experts; they made recommendations about navigation in northern waters to the American and Canadian governments: *http://byers.typepad.com/arctic/model-negotiation-on-northern-waters.html*.)

Evaluate the research work of each individual student when completed.

Step Six

When their research is complete, have the students gather as a class to discuss their evaluations. Ask: Who decided the governance structure in place is adequate? Who decided it needed changes?

If there are students who decided the governance structure is adequate, have them be first to share their evaluations. Have the other pairs of students share next.

Encourage the class to discuss similarities and differences in evaluations and summarize the various points of view. If possible, have them reach a consensus on their views.

OPTIONAL EXTENSION ACTIVITIES

- Students may research if any countries are making a claim to sovereignty over the North Pole and if not, why not.

- Pairs of students can look up, and read, "A Circumpolar Inuit Declaration on Sovereignty in the Arctic." (Some of them may have read Section 1 as an extension activity for Lesson One.) They can summarize the main points and prepare a poster, presenting the views of this group of Inuit on "Action for the North."

- In his 2006 speech in Iqaluit, Nunavut on the topic of Canada's North, Prime Minister Harper said: "Canada's Arctic sovereignty is firmly anchored in history. Almost 100 years ago, in 1909, a plaque was installed on Melville Island by famed Quebecois seaman Joseph Bernier, captain of the Canadian government ship Arctic. It proclaimed, on the ground for the first time, Canada's sovereignty over the entire Arctic Archipelago. From the 1920s through the 1940s, the great Canadian navigator Henry Larsen patrolled our Arctic waters aboard the famous RCMP schooner St. Roch. Larsen's many voyages upheld the first principle of Arctic sovereignty: Use it or lose it." Verify Prime Minister Harper's statements about history, and after conducting research, make a timeline showing other Canadian activity in the North that bolsters Canada's claim to "using" it.

- Students can investigate the Arctic Water Pollution Prevention Act, for example, when it was enacted and why, and, in particular, assess reasons for renewed political interest in the law.

- Students may research the Radarsat-2 and its impact on Canada's North. In particular, they can look at why the government blocked the sale of the satellite (in April 2008) and what mechanism allowed this government action. (This was the first time Canada blocked the sale of a domestic firm to a foreign buyer.) Have them investigate other examples of government intervening in international deals.

- Students may write a letter to the Prime Minister suggesting the implementation of measures they believe the Canadian government should be pursuing in order to maintain sovereignty in the Arctic while following the existing laws and conventions of governance. Remind them to write in a formal style, to check their sources and the accuracy of any facts they present, and to provide supporting evidence for their comments. Suggest that they ask for a reply.

ASSESSMENT AND EVALUATION RUBRICS

General

Discussion
Level 1   Did not participate or contribute to the teacher-directed discussions
Level 2   Participated somewhat in the teacher-directed discussions
Level 3   Actively participated in the teacher-directed discussions
Level 4   Made a significant contribution to the teacher-directed discussions

Content
Level 1   Demonstrated limited understanding of concepts, facts, and terms
Level 2   Demonstrated some understanding of concepts, facts, and terms
Level 3   Demonstrated considerable understanding of concepts, facts, and terms
Level 4   Demonstrated thorough understanding of concepts, facts, and terms

Written Work
Level 1   Written report had many grammatical errors, is poorly structured and confusing
Level 2   Written report was generally clear, but has numerous grammatical errors
Level 3   Written report was well-structured and clear, but has a few significant/ grammatical errors
Level 4   Written report was very clear, well-organized with few errors

Oral Presentation
Level 1   Oral report was confusing, lacked emphasis and energy, with no discussion resulting
Level 2   Oral report was adequate, but lacked emphasis and energy, with little discussion resulting
Level 3   Oral report was clear and well presented, but lacked some emphasis and energy with a good discussion resulting
Level 4   Oral report was clear and enthusiastically presented, with energetic discussion resulting

Teamwork
Level 1   1 or 2 members dominated the team, very little cooperation
Level 2   Majority of the group made a contribution with some recognition of individual strengths, but cooperation was superficial
Level 3   Most members made a significant contribution, with a good level of cooperation
Level 4   All members made a significant contribution, individual strengths were recognized and used effectively, excellent co-operation among group members

Specific

Step One
Level 1   Student demonstrated a poor understanding of governance
Level 2   Student demonstrated a basic understanding of governance
Level 3   Student demonstrated a good understanding of governance
Level 4   Student demonstrated an exemplary understanding of governance

Step Two

Level 1   Student demonstrated a poor understanding of sovereignty and its implications

Level 2   Student demonstrated a basic understanding of sovereignty and its implications

Level 3   Student demonstrated a good understanding of sovereignty and its implications

Level 4   Student demonstrated an exemplary understanding of sovereignty and its implications

Step Three

Level 1   Student exhibited a poor understanding of measures that could strengthen the government's claims to the North

Level 2   Student exhibited a basic understanding of measures that could strengthen the government's claims to the North

Level 3   Student exhibited a good understanding of measures that could strengthen the government's claims to the North

Level 4   Student exhibited an exemplary understanding of measures that could strengthen the government's claims to the North

Step Four

Level 1   Student demonstrated a poor ability to suggest key questions to aid analysis

Level 2   Student demonstrated a basic ability to propose key questions to aid analysis

Level 3   Student demonstrated a good ability to propose key questions to aid analysis

Level 4   Student demonstrated an exemplary ability to propose key questions to aid analysis

Step Five

Level 1   Student demonstrated poor research skills

Level 2   Student demonstrated basic research skills

Level 3   Student demonstrated good research skills

Level 4   Student demonstrated exemplary research skills

Step Six

Level 1   Student exhibited a poor ability to evaluate existing Arctic governance structure and suggest alternative

Level 2   Student exhibited a basic ability to evaluate existing Arctic governance structure and suggest alternative

Level 3   Student exhibited a good ability to evaluate existing Arctic governance structure and suggest alternative

Level 4   Student exhibited an exemplary ability to evaluate existing Arctic governance structure and suggest alternative

RESOURCES

General info on Canadian International Law
www.canadianlawsite.ca/international.htm

"Fund Inuit, not Canadian, Arctic sovereignty" (Marie Wadden article in The Globe and Mail, Aug. 2009)
www.theglobeandmail.com/globe-debate/fund-inuit-not-canadian-arctic-sovereignty/article4214072

"Canadian sovereignty over Arctic waters on thin ice" (July 2007 article)
http://en.epochtimes.com/news/7-7-12/57562.html

Canadian sovereignty in the Artic: Challenges for the RCMP
(June 2007-Archived content)
www.rcmp-grc.gc.ca/ci-rc/reports-rapports/cs-sc/index-eng.htm

"Harper aims to widen Canada's arctic sovereignty" (Aug. 2008 article, Toronto Star)
www.thestar.com/news/2008/08/27/harper_aims_to_widen_canadas_arctic_sovereignty.html

"For Sale : Arctic Sovereignty?" (June 2008 article in The Walrus)
http://thewalrus.ca/for-sale-arctic-sovereignty

North American Integration and the Militarization of the Arctic
(Aug. 2007 article):
www.globalresearch.ca/index.php?context=va&aid=6586

The Race to the Arctic and International Law (blog)
http://itssdjournalunclos-lost.blogspot.com/2008/05/httpwww.html

China Prepares for an Ice-free Arctic (article)
http://books.sipri.org/files/insight/SIPRIInsight1002.pdf

The Danish Continental Shelf Project (website)
http://a76.dk/lng_uk/main.html

UNCLOS (United Nations Convention on the Law of the Sea)
www.un.org/Depts/los/convention_agreements/texts/unclos/closindx.htm

Oceans & Law of the Sea—United Nations:
www.un.org/Depts/los/index.htm

LESSON THREE: CITIZENSHIP AND CANADA'S NORTH

DURATION:

Five to Eight classroom periods

CURRICULUM LINKS:

Social Studies
World History
World Geography
(For specific curriculum links, please visit www.teachmag.com/curricula)

The goal is for students to reflect on their understanding of the concept of citizenship and then to apply it to the issues related to Canada's North, including Canada's sovereignty in the North. Students will review the rights and responsibilities that they share with all Canadians, and discuss why being an active citizen is important. They will discuss the changing face of democracy and how technological tools can increase the abilities of citizens to meaningfully participate in the process. They will co-operate to plan and put into action an Anti-Apathy Campaign. This project engages students in encouraging their fellow students to participate in the democratic process by accessing information, and voicing their concerns about "big issues," such as sovereignty in the Arctic, by using online tools. Together, they will try to stimulate a "buzz" about Canada's North in order to express their opinions, and, in so doing, perhaps influence one another and their government representatives.

They will read (or reread) the pages in the graphic novel, *Project North: Canadian Sovereignty in the Arctic*, describing what Alex and ZaZi learn about the connection between citizenship and sovereignty in the north.

MATERIALS REQUIRED

- Computers, tablets, or mobile devices with Internet access
- Detailed map of Canada's North:
  http://maps.nationalgeographic.com/maps/atlas/north-america-geophysical.html
- Writing paper and tools, computers, or mobile devices
- Graphic novel *Project North: Canadian Sovereignty in the Arctic* available to download for free at www.teachmag.com/cnp

KEY CONCEPTS AND ISSUES

Students will explore the concept of citizenship and how it connects to issues related to it.

EXPECTATIONS/OUTCOMES

Students will:
- Identify and explain the rights and responsibilities of individual citizens in a local, national, and global context
- Demonstrate an understanding of the need for democratic decision-making
- Analyze a contemporary crisis or issue of international significance (e.g., Canada's sovereignty in the Arctic)
- Recognize the difficulties in prioritizing global issues

- Evaluate the impact of some technological developments on Canadians in different periods
- Take age-appropriate actions to demonstrate their responsibilities as citizens

BACKGROUND

The country with sovereignty in the Arctic region will have significant benefits. Canadian sovereignty in the North is being challenged by many Arctic countries, including the United States, Russia, Iceland, Denmark, Finland, Norway, and Sweden. Students have learned about and researched the issue in Lessons One and Two and will understand that Canada must take a leadership role in preserving, and continuing to assert, its sovereignty in the North.

This focus of the project is students motivating other students to get involved in participatory democracy by using the tools available to them through the Internet. (Remind students to be cautious in accessing sites and review with them the rules of appropriate and safe Internet use.) Some of the tools are: social networking sites such as Facebook, Twitter, Instagram, and Snapchat.

Step One: Teacher-Led Discussion

Begin with a general discussion about citizenship and what it is. Ask students to suggest the roles and responsibilities of a Canadian citizen.

According to Citizenship and Immigration Canada, "everyone in Canada has rights and responsibilities. These are based on Canadian laws and shared values. Many of these rights are defined in the Canadian Charter of Rights and Freedoms."

They describe some of the rights of a Canadian citizen as:
- Legal rights
- Equality rights
- Mobility rights
- Aboriginal peoples' rights
- Freedom of thought
- Freedom of speech
- Freedom of religion
- The right to peaceful assembly

They describe some of the responsibilities of a Canadian citizen as:
- To obey Canada's laws
- To express opinions freely while respecting the rights and freedoms of others
- To help others in the community
- To care for and protect our heritage and environment
- To eliminate discrimination and injustice

Have them discuss the rights and responsibilities of citizens in a local, national, and global context. Review with students the importance of the North to Canada and remind them that other nations are challenging Canada's claim to the Arctic. Have them review (from Lesson Two) what Canada is doing to ensure it maintains its presence in the Arctic.

Have students read on in the graphic novel *Project North: Canadian Sovereignty in the Arctic* to learn more about citizenship and Canada's North.

Step Two

Do a secret survey, asking students to indicate:
- Whether or not they care about Canada's sovereignty in the North
- Whether or not they want to do something about helping protect our heritage in the North

Have volunteers tally the results and report them to the class.

Initiate a class discussion about participatory democracy, specifically focussing on whether or not they think Canadian youth are active as citizens. Discuss some reasons why youth might not feel interested in world issues, or even in events or challenges being faced by Canadians (ignorance of issues, overwhelmed by number of issues and magnitude of media news, issues are "boring" and not connected to lives of youth, difficult to prioritize issues, issues are generalized and "dumbed down" in the media and no analysis is provided). Discuss some reasons why youth might not feel connected to the political process in Canada (not old enough to vote yet, sense of futility in ability to make a difference, lack of inspiring leadership, ignorance of issues, ignorance of where and how to become involved).

Ask:
- Should citizens be more involved in their democracy?
- Why is it important to share your political, and social, views?

Suggest to students that, as citizens, they have a responsibility to care for, and protect, our heritage and environment, including Canada's North. Remind them that they have learned a lot about this issue and perhaps have formed opinions. Taking a stand and making their voices heard are ways they can make a difference; they can influence decision-making and create change in a democracy. Apathy is not an option! Explain that all youth have a responsibility to get involved, and tell them that this lesson will focus on the question: How can we use modern communications technology to get more involved in protecting our heritage, specifically our connection to the North, and how can we help stimulate other youth to learn about the issue and get active too? How can we get a "buzz" going about Canada's sovereignty in the North?

Step Three

Begin by having a discussion about how technology has changed, and continues to change, the face of democracy. For example, explain that the advent of newspapers and, later, radio, and, later, television, changed the politicians' ability to reach a wider public. Have them reflect on what type of impact these media might have made in each instance (For example, ask: What would it be like to read the exact words made in a leader's speech? What would it be like to hear the actual voice of a political candidate? What would it be like for the population of a country to be able to view a live political debate simultaneously?)

Encourage students to do research and make a timeline of technological tools used to inform and influence citizens about political and social matters. For example, in 1955, the CBC televised the Opening of Parliament for the first time; in 1960, the first televised presidential debate took place between John F. Kennedy and Richard Nixon; in 1961, John F. Kennedy was the first president to hold a press conference on television; in 2006, Twitter was created and it began being used for political campaigning; the Canadian prime minister began posting weekly podcasts on his government website to communicate to citizens; in March, 2010, Stephen Harper did a YouTube interview, responding to questions submitted by Canadians to YouTube. More recently, Twitter has been used to organize, rally, and schedule political protests.

Gather together as a class and ask: Is technology changing the face of democracy, and, if so, how?

Read these three quotes to the students, and discuss:

"Yet another attempt from Stephen Harper to avoid the real media and try to control his message from the safe confines of a one-way podcast."
– 'Bankboy,' a user comment on iTunes in response to a podcast by Stephen Harper[1]

"It's a refreshing change to see a Prime Minister trying to reach out to the public and in this case a younger audience."
– 'Maple Leaf,' a user comment on iTunes in response to a podcast by Stephen Harper[2]

"What we have to do is deliver to people the best and freshest most relevant information possible. We think of Twitter as it's not a social network, but it's an information network. It tells people what they care about as it is happening in the world."
– Evan Williams, CEO of Twitter[3]

---

[1] *www.canada.com/topics/technology/story.html?id=715399bf-d927-42ee-be29-6a2d87f120d6&k=80553*
[2] *www.canada.com/topics/technology/story.html?id=715399bf-d927-42ee-be29-6a2d87f120d6&k=80553*
[3] *www.en.wikipedia.org/wiki/Twitter*

Tell students that when Stephen Harper agreed to an interview on YouTube, a total of 5,128 people cast 170,000 votes on 1,797 questions submitted by Canadians. Ask them to evaluate these results.

Gather as a group and make a chart listing the tools. Have students assess the success of these tools by asking questions such as:
- What is the impact of technological communication developments on Canadian participatory democracy in different periods?
- Do the modern tools provide a one-way message, or offer a two-way dialogue?
- How do you assess the ability of each of these modern tools to provide youth with information?
- How can youth use technological tools to become more involved in democracy?

Step Four

Tell students they will launch an Anti-Apathy Campaign to help rally youth to become active around the issue of sovereignty in Canada's North. Explain that they will have several hours throughout the weeks ahead to work on the campaign.

If you wish, share these suggestions from Mary Simon, former president of the Inuit Tapiriit Kanatami (ITK), about what people can do to help resolve the issues in the North:

"... [C]ontinue to inform yourselves ... about the Arctic. Visiting websites, including for example that of Inuit Tapiriit Kanatami (ITK), is a good start. The ITK recently provided Government with an Inuit Action Plan. ... You will find this on our website. I encourage you to read it. Being better informed you will be better placed to hold decisions-makers to account. Begin to ask questions. Within your sphere of influence, take up Arctic issues. Communicate to your family ... and governments your interest in the Arctic. Read government, Inuit, and international agency reports. They are numerous and most are available on the Internet. Contact your member of Parliament. Tell that person you want to see more discussion in Parliament about what is important to you regarding the Arctic."

Assist them in discussing and mapping out the general format of the campaign, for example, by asking questions such as:

- What are your goals for the campaign? (To educate youth about Canada's Arctic and help provide analysis about the issues; to motivate them to become involved in taking action and provide some tips about what they can do; to get youth to prioritize this issue; to get a "buzz" going on the issue)
- How will you go about achieving these goals? (Work in small groups, each one with a different technological tool; decide what key information to present and make sure it is analytical and not "dumbed-down") What technological tools that we discussed will you use, and why? (Communicate with others by making a website, blog, posting to social media networks, or publishing a video to YouTube

that address the group's views about Canada's political status in the North and Arctic sovereignty)
- Is your plan realistic?
- How will you know if your plan has been successful? (Ask for online responses, survey level of interest/concern before and after campaign, tally number of fans that sign up to website group, "likes" on Facebook, followers on Twitter, number of views on YouTube video, recognize that it may take time for the "buzz" to build momentum)

Assist the students in setting out an agenda of the tasks to be performed before the campaign launch. Have them agree on the dates by which the tasks need to be completed, the date of the launch, and the date on which they agree that they can determine the success of the campaign.

Step Five

Give students sufficient time to meet in their groups and complete their Anti-Apathy Campaign assignments.

If needed, guide them in considering how to organize, record, and present information about Canadian sovereignty in the Arctic and tips about how to get involved in the issue so it "grabs" the audience (other youth), and can be accessed readily and directly. Encourage them to think creatively while still being practical.

Monitor teamwork, and encourage each student to share their skills (which may vary widely).

Step Six

Assist students in launching the Anti-Apathy Campaign on the designated day.

After the time allotted, meet again as a class. Discuss as a class the results of the Anti-Apathy Campaign. Help the students evaluate the process they created, and establish whether the final goals were met. Have them think about what they might do differently next time. Ask them to share comments about how it felt to try to motivate others to become more involved in Canada's democracy and what they learned from this experience.

OPTIONAL EXTENSION ACTIVITIES

- In his article, "Thank You for Not Voting," Will Wilkinson, a research fellow at the Cato Institute in Washington, DC., argues that low voter turnout can signal social solidarity, reflect real civic virtue, and even make democracy work better. For example, he claims that "lower levels of turnout may suggest that voters actually trust each other more—that fewer feel an urgent need to vote defensively, to guard against competing interests or ideologies." He also states, "If well-informed voters have a better picture of the candidate or party most likely to promote the general welfare, then especially high turnout can actually tilt an election away from the better choice, leaving everyone a bit worse off." Have students in small groups discuss these ideas and give an opinion about them. Then encourage them to research, to find, and read, online this particular article or other materials on this topic. Have them gather again to discuss what they have found out and whether their views have changed.

- Students can watch the first Kennedy-Nixon debate (and, if possible, the three that followed), and write their reflections. Who do they think "won" the debates, and why? Then research to find out the response of the general public at the time. What does this tell them about the media and the impressions made by political leaders?

- Students can consider how blogging is used in politics and political campaigns, for example, they can listen to former Conservative Alberta MP Monte Solberg's comments about blogging being "the newest tool in politics" and why he believes it is becoming more popular. (He used blogs to communicate with his constituents about "the inside things that occur on Parliament Hill" and also because it's "fun.")

Students can check out the Apathy is Boring website to compare the suggestions offered there to strategies adopted by the student groups in the class. Have them write a short paragraph assessing the site.

ASSESSMENT AND EVALUATION RUBRICS

General

Discussion
Level 1   Did not participate or contribute to the teacher-directed discussions
Level 2   Participated somewhat in the teacher-directed discussions
Level 3   Actively participated in the teacher-directed discussions
Level 4   Made a significant contribution to the teacher-directed discussions

Content
Level 1   Demonstrated limited understanding of concepts, facts, and terms
Level 2   Demonstrated some understanding of concepts, facts, and terms
Level 3   Demonstrated considerable understanding of concepts, facts, and terms
Level 4   Demonstrated thorough understanding of concepts, facts, and terms

Written Work

Level 1   Written report had many grammatical errors, is poorly structured and confusing

Level 2   Written report was generally clear, but has numerous grammatical errors

Level 3   Written report was well-structured and clear, but has a few significant/ grammatical errors

Level 4   Written report was very clear, well-organized with few errors

Oral Presentation

Level 1   Oral report was confusing, lacked emphasis and energy, with no discussion resulting

Level 2   Oral report was adequate, but lacked emphasis and energy. with little discussion resulting

Level 3   Oral report was clear and well presented, but lacked some emphasis and energy with a good discussion resulting

Level 4   Oral report was clear and enthusiastically presented, with energetic discussion resulting

Teamwork

Level 1   1 or 2 members dominated the team, very little cooperation

Level 2   Majority of the group made a contribution with some recognition of individual strengths, but cooperation was superficial

Level 3   Most members made a significant contribution, with a good level of cooperation

Level 4   All members made a significant contribution, individual strengths were recognized and used effectively, excellent co-operation among group members

Specific

Step One

Level 1   Student has a poor understanding of citizenship and global citizenship

Level 2   Student has a basic understanding of citizenship and global citizenship

Level 3   Student has a good understanding of citizenship and global citizenship

Level 4   Student has an exemplary understanding of citizenship and global citizenship

Step Two

Level 1   Student demonstrated poor participation in discussion about participatory democracy

Level 2   Student demonstrated basic participation in discussion about participatory democracy

Level 3   Student demonstrated good participation in discussion about participatory democracy

Level 4   Student demonstrated exemplary participation in discussion about participatory democracy

Step Three
Level 1   Student has a poor ability to assess the impact of technological communication developments on Canadian participatory democracy
Level 2   Student has a basic ability to assess the impact of technological communication developments on Canadian participatory democracy
Level 3   Student has a good ability to assess the impact of technological communication developments on Canadian participatory democracy
Level 4   Student has an exemplary ability to assess the impact of technological communication developments on Canadian participatory democracy

Step Four
Level 1   Student exhibited poor participation in the planning of the Anti-Apathy Campaign
Level 2   Student exhibited basic participation in the planning of the Anti-Apathy Campaign
Level 3   Student exhibited good participation in the planning of the Anti-Apathy Campaign
Level 4   Student exhibited exemplary participation in the planning of the Anti-Apathy Campaign

Step Five
Level 1   Student exhibited poor teamwork and sharing of skills in preparing the Anti-Apathy Campaign materials
Level 2   Student exhibited basic teamwork and sharing of skills in preparing the Anti-Apathy Campaign materials
Level 3   Student exhibited good teamwork and sharing of skills in preparing the Anti-Apathy Campaign materials
Level 4   Student exhibited exemplary teamwork and sharing of skills in preparing the Anti-Apathy Campaign materials

Step Six
Level 1   Student came away with a poor understanding of the results of the Anti-Apathy Campaign
Level 2   Student came away with a basic understanding of the results of the Anti-Apathy Campaign
Level 3   Student came away with a good understanding of the results of the Anti-Apathy Campaign
Level 4   Student came away with an exemplary understanding of the results of the Anti-Apathy Campaign

RESOURCES

Information about becoming a Canadian citizen
www.cic.gc.ca/english/citizenship/index.asp

Canadian non-partisan organization
www.apathyisboring.com

Canadian Prime Minister's webpage with links to Twitter feed, YouTube channel, Flickr account, and podcasts
www.pm.gc.ca

Kennedy/Nixon debate, 1960 (Part 1)
www.archive.org/details/1960_kennedy-nixon_1
www.youtube.com/results?search_query=nixon-kennedy+debate

First televised American news conference (Jan 25, 1961)
www.youtube.com/results?search_query=nixon-kennedy+debate

First podcast report from Capital Hill, Ottawa, 2005
www.politicswatch.com/what%20is%20podcasting.mp3

Apathy is Boring
www.apathyisboring.com/en/the_facts/articles/48

Canada's World website
www.canadasworld.ca

Former MP Monte Solberg's comments on blogging as the newest political tool
www.politicswatch.com/solberg-blog-may27-2005.mp3

LESSON FOUR: DIVERSITY AND CANADA'S NORTH

DURATION:

Five to Eight classroom periods

CURRICULUM LINKS:

Social Studies
World History
World Geography
(For specific curriculum links, please visit *www.teachmag.com/curricula*)

Although historically isolated from the rest of the country, the North has nevertheless contributed in a powerful way to the Canadian national identity. Canada stretches from sea to sea to sea and Canadian citizens, no matter what part of the country they inhabit, have a bond with their fellow Canadians in the North that needs to be acknowledged and celebrated.

Students will reflect on their understanding of the concept of diversity and apply it to the issues related to Canada's North. They will try to view Canada's struggle for sovereignty in the North through the perspectives of various Canadian communities and evaluate its significance for them and for the nation. By participating in this activity, students will develop their thinking about Canada's identity as a nation of diverse peoples and how it is possible for issues, such as Canada's North, to unite citizens.

They will read the chapter in the graphic novel, *Project North: Canadian Sovereignty in the Arctic* that describes what Alex and ZaZi learn about diversity and sovereignty in the North as they do their school project.

KEY CONCEPTS AND ISSUES

Students will explore the concept of diversity and how it connects to issues relating to Canada's North. Subjects: Diversity and Canada's North.

MATERIALS REQUIRED

- Computers or mobile devices with Internet access
- Detailed map of Canada's North:
  http://maps.nationalgeographic.com/maps/atlas/north-america-geophysical.html
- Writing paper and tools, computers, or mobile devices
- Graphic novel *Project North: Canadian Sovereignty in the Arctic* available to download for free at *www.teachmag.com/cnp*

EXPECTATIONS/OUTCOMES

Students will:
- Demonstrate an understanding of the beliefs and values underlying democratic citizenship and explain how they guide citizens' actions
- Describe the diversity of beliefs and values of various individuals and groups in Canadian society
- Analyze responses at the local, national, and international levels to civic issues that involve multiple perspectives and differing civic purposes

- Compare the varied beliefs, values, and points of view of Canadian citizens on issues of public interest (e.g., freedom of information, censorship, health-care funding, pollution, water quality, nuclear power, taxation, casinos, sovereignty in the North)
- Analyze Canadian issues or events that involve contrasting opinions, perspectives, and civic purposes (e.g., Canada's efforts to maintain sovereignty in the North)
- Describe how their own and others' beliefs and values can be connected to a sense of civic purpose and preferred types of participation (e.g., membership in political parties; participation in protest movements; financial or volunteer support for educational or community service programs; support for religious or ethnic charitable organizations)

BACKGROUND

Step One: Teacher-Led Discussion

Remind students of the beliefs and values underlying democratic citizenship and explain how they guide citizens' actions. Have students discuss the concept of diversity as it applies to Canadian society. Explain how different groups (e.g., special interest groups, ethno-cultural groups) define their citizenship, and identify the beliefs and values reflected in these definitions. Have students share information, if they wish, about their own backgrounds, beliefs, and values.

Ask how diversity might co-exist with the values of democratic citizenship.

Have students read on in *Project North: Canadian Sovereignty in the Arctic*.

Step Two

Brainstorm a list of issues of public interest to Canadians (e.g., freedom of information, censorship, health-care funding, pollution, water quality, nuclear power, taxation, casinos, military defense), and ask students what they know of the varied beliefs, values, and points of view that Canadian citizens might have on these issues.

Then, if they have not suggested it, mention Canada's sovereignty in the North as an issue of public interest. Tell them that in our society that celebrates diverse interests and points of view, different people might have varying perspectives on Arctic sovereignty. Ask students to discuss varied beliefs, values, and points of view of Canadian citizens on this issue (its importance and how it is to be achieved). They may vary in
- What it means to them
- Their assessment of its importance to the country
- Whether it should be important to more citizens (whether more Canadians should care about Arctic sovereignty) and if so, why?

(If necessary, refer them back to Lessons One and Two for an example of one perspective, the perspective of the Inuit peoples. Other groups with different perspectives could include local and regional authorities, NGOs promoting environmental protection, commercial interests (including large energy companies, fishing interests, shipping companies, tourist businesses), provincial, territorial, and federal governments (which might also have interests in the energy companies), and government organizations, such as the Canadian Armed Forces. If you wish, have students read "Opinion: Canada and the Northwest Passage – Sovereignty versus Heritage," a January 2009 article which mentions different stakeholders and their perspectives.)

Use several or all of the following quotes to continue to stimulate discussion about different perspectives and the diversity of interests. (Either post them, circulate them on paper, or read them aloud.)

"Diplomacy may be cheaper than employing naval forces, but it will probably be inadequate. The demand for energy worldwide will continue and there will be shortages. The small and medium powers are likely the most at risk. ... Most small- and medium-sized coastal states are, therefore, not relying on diplomacy alone. ... In Canada and the United States, there are regular suggestions that the NORAD surveillance effort be extended into this region. In such cooperative endeavours, Canada must remember that one's voice is precisely proportional to the strength of one's military contribution."
– Eric Lehre, excerpt from "Future Canadian Security Challenges and Some Responses," in Canadian Naval Review, Winter 2010

"From Canadians' point of view this is an opportunity that will never come again."
– Ruth Jackson of the Geological Survey of Canada, in reference to Canada's opportunity to extend its territory further under its coastal waters by providing scientific evidence (that the formations are geologically connected to its mainland) to a United Nations commission by 2013

"It's our home. It's not some new frontier. It's not some new frontier just to be explored. This is our homeland. For us it's a way of life that we're protecting."
– Sheila Watt-Cloutier, Inuit activist who was nominated in 2007 for the Nobel Peace Prize

"The Arctic is rapidly becoming subject to plans involving shipping, expanded industry, and national security. While Canada appears to be gearing up for the challenge, will the traditionally docile Canadian population have the gumption to support the pursuit of the country's northern interests?"
– Neil Hazan, lawyer, excerpt from "Asserting Ourselves (in the Arctic)," June 2009

"Arctic exploration and development will create needed economic opportunities for northern communities, help secure Canada's energy supply and provide an opportunity for Canada to clearly exercise its economic sovereignty over offshore natural resources."

– Patricia Valladao, a spokeswoman for Canada's Department of Indian & Northern Affairs, 2007[1]

"Canadians should stop worrying about our Arctic possessions and instead move forward in building an Arctic in which all exercise proper care in the enjoyment and exploitation of a shared environment. We should be aiming for co-operative stewardship as well as national sovereignty. Academics and others whom I call "purveyors of polar peril" have helped politicians and the media persuade us we have far greater sovereignty problems than we actually do. "Use it or lose it" typifies the misguided thinking of southerners who, removed from Arctic realities, seek to maintain remote control over the North.

Stewardship means locally informed governance that not only polices, but also cares for and respects, the natural environment and all living things in it, humans included. Stewardship cannot be done in isolation. In the Arctic it requires not only national but international co-operation. Leadership for co-operative stewardship should come from Northerners in Canada, from those who know the region best and are uniquely positioned to bring a circumpolar perspective to the politics of Canada's Arctic policies.

We should come out of the shell of our concern for sovereignty and start to act like sovereigns. We need to join with others in the region and take care before it's too late for the Arctic."

– Franklyn Griffith, Professor Emeritus of political science and George Ignatieff Chair emeritus of peace and conflict studies at the University of Toronto

"We could ... declare[e] the North the largest national park on Earth. Imagine a terrestrial and marine protected area encompassing the 3.5 million square kilometres of the Yukon, NWT, Nunavut and the waters that lie between the 60th parallel and the pole. ... The park's only restrictions on resource extraction would be on fossil fuels. Why? Because everyone knows climate change is undermining the ecology of the North, where the warming is three times the global average. What better way to signal our opposition to business-as-usual than making oil and gas reserves in the North off limits?

*According to the U.S. Geological Survey, **90 billion barrels** of oil lie untapped north of the Arctic Circle. That's a **10th** of known conventional reserves. More than **30 per cent** of the world's undiscovered natural gas may be there too. Take it all away and everyone – especially the Russian and Danish diplomats now*

---

1 *www.upstreamonline.com/live/article156093.ece?service=print*

arguing with Canada over drilling rights to the Arctic Ocean's Lomonosov Ridge, northwest of Greenland – will take us seriously. They'll object, but at least Canada will be negotiating from the moral high ground. Indeed, transforming Canada's North into one big park may be the most powerful action we can take to address global warming."
– James Hrynyshyn, a Canadian science journalist based in North Carolina

"It's been years since the North dominated headlines like it does today. Questions about sovereignty, resources, and national boundaries have all raised people's attention. But the nature of the debate, dominated by southern surprise that the North is of international importance, has revealed a paradox. Canada, though Northern, is not yet a truly Northern nation.

My greatest wish is for our country to realize the uniqueness of its North. ... [I]f Canada were a Northern nation, we'd never have endless debates about Arctic sovereignty. We don't obsess about the future of B.C. or ponder challenges to the geographical integrity of Manitoba. The North would have a permanent place in the national fabric and would not be subject to cyclical interest and southern neglect. To become a Northern nation, Canadians need to overcome their inherent bias against winter and cold, and move beyond mythology toward a sophisticated understanding of the North. The Arctic and Subarctic must cease to be foreign territories hidden by distance and climate, and instead must be seen as a viable, appealing and utterly normal part of Canada."
– Ken Coates, a writer raised in the Yukon and Dean of Arts at the University of Waterloo

"As exchanges between Prime Minister Harper and the U.S. ambassador revealed last fall, much of the government rhetoric about Arctic security is confrontational, pitting Canada against the United States and stressing our divergent interests. But there may also be opportunities for cooperation, as our study of the DEW Line experience reveals. The Rangers [a community volunteer component of the Canadian Forces Reserves, of which two-thirds are of Aboriginal descent] demonstrate that there is also room for intimate cooperation and practical partnership within our diverse country. ... While the existing literature tends to stress points of friction between Aboriginal peoples and the Canadian military, such as confrontations at Goose Bay, Oka, and Ipperwash, there is also intimate cooperation and very positive relationships that prevail across the North. We sometimes forget that Inuit leaders have defined themselves as 'Canadian First, First Canadians.'"
– Whitney Lackenbauer, Assistant Professor at University of Waterloo, who studies sovereignty and security in The North, 2006

Review each quote, reflecting on the content of the opinion, whose opinion it is and how one could categorize the speaker (i.e., What "interest group" does the speaker belong to?).

Step Three

Explain to students that throughout Canada's history, one of the challenges has been to establish a sense of national identity in a vast country that stretches from sea to sea to sea. Remind them that citizens do not always agree on how to handle public issues or even on the importance of public issues.

Post this poll, or read it to the students (from a February 2007 AngusReid about Canadian Arctic sovereignty):

Q: On a scale of 1 to 10, how important is the issue of Arctic sovereignty to Canada?
Important - 48%
Neutral - 18%
Not important - 9%
Don't know - 24%

The importance of this issue is felt more strongly among older Canadians aged 55 or older: 64%, 35-54: 49%, under 35: 34%), those with a post-secondary education (51% vs. 40% of those without) and men (60% vs. 37% of women).

Q: In your opinion, is Canada's northern border most vulnerable to...
Usage of natural resources - 57%
American control - 36%
Terrorist attacks - 10%
Enemy nations making land claims - 9%
Don't know/refused - 9%
None of the above - 5%

Younger Canadians (under 35: 61%, 35-54: 57%) are most concerned with the usage of natural resources, while the fears of those over 54 are split between American control (43%) and the use of natural resources (51%).

Q: Which of the following statements would you most agree with?
Canada should assert its Arctic sovereignty claims through legal authority - 52%
Canada should assert its Arctic sovereignty claims by placing troops at key points - 18%
Canada should assert its existing practices as they relate to Arctic sovereignty - 12%
Canada should not worry about Arctic sovereignty - 4%
Don't know/refused - 15%

Discuss with the students how the respondents are divided into age categories. Ask whether this might affect their responses.

Share this poll (that compares August 2007 views to August 2008 views):

Polling Data

Do you agree or disagree with the following statements?
(Strongly Agree / Moderately Agree responses only)

	Aug. 2008	Aug. 2007
Canada should invest heavily on securing sovereignty over its Arctic territory	74%	75%
Russia represents a bigger threat than the United States to Canada in matters related to Arctic sovereignty	54%	53%
I have confidence in the government of Stephen Harper to secure Canada's Arctic sovereignty	41%	44%
Canada should plant a flag on the Arctic's seabed	56%	51%

Source: Angus Reid Strategies
Methodology: Online interviews with 1,014 Canadian adults, conducted from Aug. 15 to Aug. 17, 2008. Margin of error is 3.1 per cent.

Finally, read to students the results of this national poll released in May 2008 by the Pembina Institute:

"Twenty nine per cent of Canadians chose "global warming" when asked what the federal government's top priority should be in the Canadian Arctic. "Environmental protection" came second at 26 per cent, for a combined total of 55 per cent. Addressing social problems was respondents' third choice at 18 per cent, followed by the federal government's current focus, "Canadian sovereignty," in fourth place at 17 per cent. Just seven per cent of Canadians say that economic development is a top priority in the Arctic."[2]

Discuss these questions with the students:
- Do Canadians share the same views on the priorities in the Arctic or on the importance of Arctic sovereignty?
- Do you think this shows a difference in Canadians' beliefs or values? Are all Canadians equal stakeholders in the outcome?
- Is it essential that people must share the same perspective on a public issue in order to share a sense of nationhood? (Canadians have a tolerance for difference

---

2 *www.pembina.org/media-release/1645*, May 29, 2008

of opinion.) What is your perspective? How does it reflect your beliefs and values?
- Is it essential that all people must choose to participate in society in the same way in order for them to be "good citizens"? (There are a variety of ways in which people choose to participate: membership in political parties; participation in protest movements; financial or volunteer support for educational or community service programs; support for religious or ethnic charitable organizations.) In what way(s) do you participate?

Step Four

Tell students their challenge in this lesson is to participate in the Raise Your Profile Project. They will create various imaginary profiles, each one describing a Canadian with a particular perspective on the issue of Canadian sovereignty in The North and its importance. The profile will outline the perspective and the reasons for it. The profile will describe details about the Canadian, including name, age, gender, education, occupation or way of life, philosophical views, etc. They will come up with a way to demonstrate, using the profiles that a diversity of Canadians representing a diversity of perspectives can still make up one nation.

Explain that they will have several hours throughout the weeks ahead to work on the campaign.

Assist them in discussing and planning their project for example, by asking questions such as:
- What is the purpose of the project? (To demonstrate to one another, to other students, and to the community that the diversity of interest groups with varying perspectives about Arctic sovereignty are nevertheless united within our nation).
- How will you go about achieving these goals? (Work in small groups/pairs/individually to create profiles; two profiles per team).
- What will the profiles consist of? (Illustrations accompanied by written captions for each profile; video of characters profiled giving monologues about his/her perspective; Q and A taped interviews with individuals profiled).
- Will you connect the profiles? (Have individuals take on various profiles and debate their perspectives; use the Arctic e-Discussion (see resource list below) as a model for presenting information and differing views of various profiles on Arctic sovereignty).
- Is your plan realistic?
- How will you know if it has been successful?

Step Five

Set aside time for students to work on the Raise Your Profile Project.

Observe them as they research and prepare the profiles. Evaluate how well they work together, sharing ideas, and delegating tasks. Listen in on their conversations as they assess data and decide how to present information.

Assist students in staying on target for the finish date of their project. Help them with any further preparations necessary, such as: assembling equipment or materials, inviting observers, arranging school announcements or bulletins, and/or liaising with the principal or other teachers to facilitate the participation of students in other classrooms in the school.

Step Six

Assist students in displaying or sharing their Raise Your Profile projects with the intended audience.

Step Seven

Have students discuss as a class the results of the Raise Your Profile project. Help them evaluate the process they created and establish whether the final goals were met. Have them think about what they might do differently next time. Ask them to share comments about how it felt to try to present the perspectives of others, whether or not it changed their own views, and what they learned overall from this experience.

OPTIONAL EXTENSION ACTIVITIES

- To investigate another perspective on Canada's Arctic sovereignty, students can visit the RCMP website and search for: Canadian Sovereignty in the Arctic: Challenges for the RCMP, June 5, 2007. Have them analyze the content by answering questions such as: What is the bias in this website and how do we know? Who is the audience of this website? What key points are addressed and why? What key points are not addressed and why? Have them choose a different "interest group" and create an outline of a website about Canadian Sovereignty in the Arctic that might represent this group's perspective. Ask: What do these two groups with diverse perspectives have in common? How do they both fit with one Canada?

- The year 2007-2008 was International Polar Year. The Canadian Museum of Nature hosted a series of public forums and lectures focused on the question "What does the Arctic mean to you?" Its goal was to raise national awareness about the Canadian Arctic and its people, northern issues, and the impact of climate change on polar regions. In its annual report it stated, "Events like the Polar Perspectives lecture series engaged Canadians in the debate on issues of relevance to our country's natural heritage." Students can explain whether they think this institute might have a bias, why, and what it might be. They can research to see if it has a position or perspective on Canadian sovereignty in the North. Students can consider what role Canadian institutions have in stimulating public debate in Canada, what impact they have, and what their responsibility is towards encouraging diversity and unity.

- One of the four objectives outlined in the Northern Dimension of Canada's Foreign Policy, released by the Department of Foreign Affairs and International Trade, is "to assert and ensure the preservation of Canada's sovereignty in the North." The report also states that "a Canadian strategy for a northern foreign policy was developed through a unique and extensive process of consultation with Canadians, including Aboriginal peoples, other northerners, parliamentarians, policy experts and many others. This was a deliberate process of public engagement, and one that the government intends to continue… The government believes that it is critical to maintain an ongoing process of interaction and discussion with interested stakeholders." Students can read the report, and then research to find out who exactly was consulted (who are the "stakeholders"). Have them consider why these groups were included, and whether they think there are others who should have been included in the dialogue. If so, who? Encourage them to write a letter to the organization, expressing these views and also, if they wish, their views on Canada's sovereignty in the North[5].

ASSESSMENT AND EVALUATION RUBRICS

General

Discussion
Level 1   Did not participate or contribute to the teacher-directed discussions
Level 2   Participated somewhat in the teacher-directed discussions
Level 3   Actively participated in the teacher-directed discussions
Level 4   Made a significant contribution to the teacher-directed discussions

Content
Level 1   Demonstrated limited understanding of concepts, facts, and terms
Level 2   Demonstrated some understanding of concepts, facts, and terms
Level 3   Demonstrated considerable understanding of concepts, facts, and terms
Level 4   Demonstrated thorough understanding of concepts, facts, and terms

---

[5] _www.nature.ca/pdf/ann08-09nature_e.pdf_

Written Work
Level 1 Written report had many grammatical errors, is poorly structured, and confusing
Level 2 Written report was generally clear, but has numerous grammatical errors
Level 3 Written report was well-structured and clear, but has a few significant/ grammatical errors
Level 4 Written report was very clear, well-organized with few errors

Oral Presentation
Level 1 Oral report was confusing, lacked emphasis and energy with no discussion resulting
Level 2 Oral report was adequate, but lacked emphasis and energy with little discussion resulting
Level 3 Oral report was clear and well presented, but lacked some emphasis and energy, with a good discussion resulting
Level 4 Oral report was clear and enthusiastically presented, with energetic discussion resulting

Teamwork
Level 1 1 or 2 members dominated the team, very little cooperation
Level 2 Majority of the group made a contribution with some recognition of individual strengths, but cooperation was superficial
Level 3 Most members made a significant contribution, with a good level of cooperation
Level 4 All members made a significant contribution, individual strengths were recognized and used effectively, excellent cooperation among group members

Specific

Step One
Level 1 Student has a poor understanding of diversity and democratic citizenship
Level 2 Student has a basic understanding of diversity and democratic citizenship
Level 3 Student has a good understanding of diversity and democratic citizenship
Level 4 Student has an exemplary understanding of diversity and democratic citizenship

Step Two
Level 1 Student has a poor ability to understand and compare the diversity of beliefs, values, and points of view of Canadian citizens on an issue of public interest (e.g., sovereignty in the North)
Level 2 Student has a basic ability to understand and compare the diversity of beliefs, values, and points of view of Canadian citizens on an issue of public interest (e.g., sovereignty in the North)
Level 3 Student has a good ability to understand and compare the diversity of beliefs, values, and points of view of Canadian citizens on an issue of public interest (e.g., sovereignty in the North)

Level 4   Student has an exemplary ability to understand and compare the diversity of beliefs, values, and points of view of Canadian citizens on an issue of public interest (e.g., sovereignty in the North)

Step Three
Level 1   Student has a poor understanding of how the diversity of beliefs and values of Canadian citizens, including their own, can be connected to a sense of civic purpose and preferred types of participation
Level 2   Student has a basic understanding of how the diversity of beliefs and values of Canadian citizens, including their own, can be connected to a sense of civic purpose and preferred types of participation
Level 3   Student has a good understanding of how theirs and others' beliefs and values can be connected to a sense of civic purpose and preferred types of participation
Level 4   Student has an exemplary understanding of understanding of how the diversity of beliefs and values of Canadian citizens, including their own, can be connected to a sense of civic purpose and preferred types of participation

Step Four
Level 1   Student exhibited poor participation in the planning of the Raise Your Profile project
Level 2   Student exhibited basic participation in the planning of the Raise Your Profile project
Level 3   Student exhibited good participation in the planning of the Raise Your Profile Project
Level 4   Student exhibited exemplary participation in the planning of the Raise Your Profile project

Step Five
Level 1   Student exhibited poor ability in the presentation of the Raise Your Profile project
Level 2   Student exhibited basic ability in the presentation of the Raise Your Profile project
Level 3   Student exhibited good ability in the presentation of the Raise Your Profile project
Level 4   Student exhibited exemplary ability in the presentation of the Raise Your Profile project

Step Six
Level 1   Student came away with a poor understanding of the results of the Raise Your Profile project
Level 2   Student came away with a basic understanding of the results of the Raise Your Profile project
Level 3   Student came away with a good understanding of the results of the Raise Your Profile project

Level 4   Student came away with an exemplary understanding of the results of the Raise Your Profile project

RESOURCES

Opinion: Canada and the Northwest Passage – Sovereignty versus Heritage (January 2009 opinion article)
www.digitaljournal.com/article/265204

Canada's Northern Strategy (federal government website)
www.northernstrategy.gc.ca/cns/cns-eng.asp

Northern Dimension of Canada's Foreign Policy (report)
www.canadainternational.gc.ca/eu-ue/policies-politiques/arctic-arctique.aspx?lang=eng

The Arctic: Questions and Resources (e-Discussion; Foreign Affairs, and International Trade Canada)
www.international.gc.ca/arctic-arctique/resources-ressources.aspx?lang=eng

Canadian Sovereignty in the Arctic: Challenges for the RCMP – June 5, 2007
www.rcmp-grc.gc.ca/ci-rc/reports-rapports/cs-sc/index-eng.htm

Canadian Arctic Sovereignty and Security in a Transforming Circumpolar World, Rob Huebert, July 2009 (report)
http://opencanada.org/wp-content/uploads/2011/05/Canadian-Arctic-Sovereignty-and-Security-Rob-Huebert1.pdf

= LESSON SIX

THE WELCOMING COMMUNITIES PROJECT
EXPLORING PIER 21'S HISTORY

The Welcoming Communities teaching unit thematically explores how Canada's framework of rights and obligations mitigate the effects of discrimination and racism.

GRADE LEVEL:
7 - 9

CURRICULA THEMES:

Social Studies, History, Citizenship, Global Citizenship, Civics

For a period of 43 years, Pier 21 stood as a massive gateway into Canada. It is located in Halifax, Nova Scotia and existed as the reception facility and primary point of entry that welcomed and processed visitors and hopeful citizens to this country. When it opened in 1928, the world travelled overseas by ship. But Pier 21 was more than just a disembarkation point. It was created as a modern facility welcoming some 130,000 people a year. These included evacuee children, war brides, displaced persons, refugees and new immigrants. During the war years, some 500,000 military personnel passed through its gates. Within Pier 21, visitors discovered Immigration Services, the Red Cross, Customs, Health and Welfare, Agriculture, a waiting room, dining room, canteen, nursery, hospital, kitchen and dormitories and on-site clerics to minister to the spiritual needs of those hoping to become new Canadians. Over the span of time, some one million people were welcomed to Canada when they arrived at Pier 21. The facility shut its doors permanently in 1971 when travel by ocean was overtaken by that of the airplane.

Nonetheless, Pier 21, now a museum, exists as a symbol of welcome to those who wished to come to Canada and join in its life. This country has officially created institutions and policies to help ease the transition from recent immigrant to new Canadian. It can be argued that immigration has been the lifeblood of this country and it still relies heavily on the continual influx of those who wish to settle here from other countries around the world.

As you and your students read through the stories on the Pier 21 website, you will discover that most of the newcomers' experiences in Halifax were positive. One new immigrant even recalls the Pier 21 staff greeting his children with presents upon their arrival. Certainly, coming into this large facility was disorienting for many and there were misunderstandings and confusion often due to language barriers. Even some items such as sausages were confiscated by authorities. The reminiscences generally recount a feeling of acceptance and excitement around the first days of a new and better life. Acceptance was given and barriers were lifted. Now, after passing through Pier 21, it was up to each of the families and individuals to make of Canadian life what they would. In hindsight, Pier 21 is an institution that laid the groundwork for policies and institutions that we enjoy today. Policies that embrace diversity and multiculturalism and spurn racism. Thus began a pattern that created conditions that led successive governments to enact the Canadian Charter of Rights and Freedoms and the Multiculturalism Act. Without them and Pier 21, Canada would never have won its deserved reputation as a welcoming home to peoples of the world.

The following is one example of a story of a newcomer who passed through the gates of Pier 21:

Immigrant: Antonio Saez Jiménez
Ship: Americo Vespuccio
Country: Spain

Date of Entry: September 30, 1958

Journey was from Barcelona to Lisbon to Halifax. It was terrible! Hurricane Helen, 90% of the people were sick and three old persons died.

Arrival: I remember well the ladies who came to me asking if I needed any help. I could see them helping people, old and young, taking care of babies and trying to communicate with so many Greeks and Italians who could not speak English or French. They really did do a magnificent job! Also, considering the large amounts of arrivals, the processing went smoothly and quick enough. I went right across Pier 21 to the train to Montreal and Kingston, Ontario.

I have always said that the first and main comment about the new life in, which was such a different way of living for us Mediterranean's, was that Canada gave me the same facilities Canadians born here had and to start a new life without any discrimination about nationality or language difficulties. I never felt I was living in a foreign country. Nobody is perfect but your society has something to teach others. I hope that the violent ones will always be controlled.

For personal reasons I came back to the old country. Three Canadian children, one of them remaining in Halifax, NS, with a nice Canadian wife; that is what I have given to the country that gave me manhood, with its tremendous experience.

My frequent visits to Halifax and Toronto, keeps me in constant touch with that half of myself. I am today half Spanish and half Canadian. Part of my family is in Canada and most of my friends are in Canada.

I will never forget the instant I stepped, for the first time, on Canadian soil; and when recently (2 or 3 years ago) I went back to Pier 21, so quiet and empty, I could feel the noises of children, of parents calling them in different languages. There were so many people around Pier 21 then, with the young and not so young ladies organising and helping people, so helpless many of them, and now a big empty room.

Antonio Saez Jiménez

No society is perfect, however, and exploitation of the less fortunate has and does take place (See stories on evacuee children at *www.pier21.ca*). Just as some of the evacuee children who came during the Second World War were considered by some to be cheap labour, discrimination and racism have not disappeared from our society. This is why freedoms must be protected and rights promoted in legislation such as those cited in Canadian law.

The emphasis in the lesson plan will be the acceptance of others from many different cultures and how to encourage their integration into Canadian society.

The lesson plan will also touch on issues of diversity and multiculturalism and how they strengthen the Canadian fabric.

LEARNING OUTCOMES

Students will:
- Understand the role human rights play in Canadian society
- Know that racism and discrimination violates the rights of others
- Gain an understanding of how a society is structured and functions
- How to raise awareness concerning anti-racism and human rights issues
- Work on creating a forum for the airing of a range of views relating to anti-racism and welcoming communities
- Realize that diversity is a strength when building a society
- Appreciate the role media plays in the airing of issues
- Work on collaborative learning projects
- Hone their critical assessment skills
- Work cooperatively in teams
- Assess real-world situations

BACKGROUND INFORMATION

The Canadian Charter of Rights and Freedoms

In 1982, the Canadian Charter of Rights and Freedoms came into effect. As you will see below, it is, perhaps, one of the most significant pieces of Canadian legislation currently in existence. Think back to those who came through the gates of Pier 21. Although they were welcomed to this country, laws did not yet exist that guaranteed their freedoms, enshrined their rights, and protected them from racism and discrimination. The Canadian Charter of Rights and Freedoms corrects this vital circumstance. To read the Charter in full, visit _www.pch.gc.ca_ and search for "Your Guide to the Canadian Charter of Rights and Freedoms."

What is the Canadian Charter of Rights and Freedoms?

The Canadian Charter of Rights and Freedoms is one part of the Canadian Constitution. The Constitution is a set of laws containing the basic rules about how our country operates. For example, it contains the powers of the federal government and those of the provincial governments in Canada.

The Charter sets out those rights and freedoms that Canadians believe are necessary in a free and democratic society. Some of the rights and freedoms contained in the Charter are:
- Freedom of expression
- The right to a democratic government

- The right to live and to seek employment anywhere in Canada
- Legal rights of persons accused of crimes
- Aboriginal peoples' rights
- The right to equality, including the equality of men and women
- The right to use either of Canada's official languages
- The right of French and English linguistic minorities to an education in their language
- The protection of Canada's multicultural heritage

Before the Charter came into effect, other Canadian laws protected many of the rights and freedoms that are now brought together in it. One example is the Canadian Bill of Rights, which Parliament enacted in 1960. The Charter differs from these laws by being part of the Constitution of Canada.

Who enjoys Charter rights?

Generally speaking, any person in Canada, whether a Canadian citizen, a permanent resident or a newcomer, has the rights and freedoms contained in the Charter. There are some exceptions. For example, the Charter gives some rights only to Canadian citizens—the right to vote (in section 3 of the Charter) and the right "to enter, remain in and leave Canada" (in section 6 of the Charter).

What can I do if my Charter rights have been denied?

The Charter provides for three kinds of actions to persons whose rights have been denied. These actions are referred to as legal "remedies." First, the Charter says that a person can ask a court for a remedy that is "appropriate and just in the circumstances." For instance, a court may stop proceedings against a person charged with an offence if his or her right to a trial within a reasonable time has been denied.

A second remedy is available when persons carrying out investigations for the government (for example, police officers) violate an individual's Charter rights. This may happen, for example, when they improperly search for evidence on private property and violate a person's right to privacy. In this situation, the person can ask a court to order that the evidence not be used against the person in a trial. A court will make an order like this if it is clear that using such evidence at trial would "bring the administration of justice into disrepute" (under section 24 of the Charter).

Finally, if a court finds that a law violates Charter rights, it can rule that the law has no force (under section 52 of the Constitution Act, 1982).

Universal Declaration of Human Rights
www.un.org

Before the Canadian Charter of Rights and Freedoms came into being, the United Nations passed the first charter that recognized that all peoples have rights and responsibilities. It should be noted that it was a Canadian, John Humphreys, who drafted the Universal Declaration of Human Rights. In doing so, Humphreys helped establish a foundation for the Canadian legislation.

On December 10, 1948, the General Assembly of the United Nations adopted and proclaimed the Universal Declaration of Human Rights. Following this historic proclamation, the General Assembly called upon all Member states to promote the text of the Declaration and " to cause it to be disseminated, displayed, read and expounded principally in schools and other educational institutions, without distinction based on the political status of countries or territories."

All educators and youth should familiarize themselves with the following:

Do citizens have rights? If so, what are they?

"...The General Assembly proclaims This Universal Declaration of Human Rights as a common standard of achievement for all peoples and all nations, to the end that every individual and every organ of society, keeping this Declaration constantly in mind, shall strive by teaching and education to promote respect for these rights and freedoms and by progressive measures, national and international, to secure their universal and effective recognition and observance, both among the peoples of Member States themselves and among the peoples of territories under their jurisdiction."

For example:

Article 1: *All human beings are born free and equal in dignity and rights. They are endowed with reason and conscience and should act towards one another in a spirit of brotherhood.*

Article 3: *Everyone has the right to life, liberty, and security of person.*

Article 4: *No one shall be held in slavery or servitude; slavery and the slave trade shall be prohibited in all their forms.*

Article 5: *No one shall be subjected to torture or to cruel, inhuman, or degrading treatment or punishment.*

Article 6: *Everyone has the right to recognition everywhere as a person before the law.*

Article 9: *No one shall be subjected to arbitrary arrest, detention or exile.*

In all, there are 30 Articles that comprise the Universal Declaration of Human Rights.

Every new Canadian is accorded rights in our society. It must be openly recognized that human rights take precedence and are accorded everyone. To be seen as a positive and fully functioning citizen, however, a set of responsibilities comes with those rights (see list immediately below). It is also incumbent on the communities where immigrants settle to ensure that all rights are recognized and protected just as it is incumbent on the individuals to know their rights and how to exercise them.

With rights, however, come responsibilities:
- Understand and obey societal laws
- Participate in democratic political systems
- Vote in elections
- Allow others to enjoy their rights and freedoms
- Appreciate and help preserve the world's cultural heritage
- Acquire knowledge and understanding of people and places around the world
- Become stewards of the environment
- Speak out against social injustice, discrimination and racism
- Challenge institutional thinking when it abrogates human rights

"As we enter our centennial year we are still a young nation, very much in the formative stages. Our national condition is still flexible enough that we can make almost anything we wish of our nation. No other country is in a better position than Canada to go ahead with the evolution of a national purpose devoted to all that is good and noble and excellent in the human spirit."
– Lester B. Pearson

Step One: Teacher-Led Discussion

Have each member of the class read the background information on the Canadian Charter of Rights and Freedoms and the Universal Declaration of Human Rights, on government policies such as multiculturalism and diversity. Have a discussion with the class on the importance of all of these rights within a society and in particular a country like Canada. Link the notion of human rights to anti-racism and discrimination.

This is the central question or thesis of the teaching unit: When human rights are observed, do racism and discrimination diminish, and are all peoples recognized as having an equal place in society? Talk about some of the government policies that Canada has in place that help promote multiculturalism and diversity. What sort of impact do members of the class feel these policies have had and has the impact been positive or negative? Have students give specific reasons for their answers.

Step Two: Debate the Issues

Divide the class into three and four member discussion groups. Ask half of the groups to examine and list the challenges presented by a multicultural society. Have the other groups discuss the notion that having a multicultural society delivers positive developments and have them document the benefits. Each group will appoint a spokesperson who will state the position of their group and read out the list of challenges or benefits.

The teacher will jot the Challenges and Benefits on the board for all to see. With the lists side by side, is it possible to draw any conclusions based on the two distinct lists? Overall, does the class feel that a multicultural society is a good thing or not? If there are challenges, what can be done to address them and to enhance the benefits?

EXTENSION ACTIVITIES

Students will complete at least one of the following:

Programs

Students working in groups will research successful anti-racism campaigns e.g., International Day for the Elimination of Racial Discrimination, March 21. They will prepare a brief summary on these successful programs with a view to designing and launching their own anti-racism campaign in their community. The group will select a spokesperson who will make an oral presentation to the class presenting the findings.

Resources

Canadian Heritage
www.pch.gc.ca

Mosaic BC
www.mosaicbc.com

Alternatives International
www.alternatives.ca

Expression

Students working in groups create their own public awareness campaign that promotes one of the key themes within social interactions like anti-racism. Students may choose the format in which they wish to work, e.g., print, audio, video, animation, blog, etc. Each member of the group is assigned a task and a timeline in which to complete it.

Resources

Media Smarts
www.mediasmarts.ca

Simulation

Students work in groups to create their own society, develop specific charters, laws, policies, programs and citizenship values. Existing societal models may be researched and include: Democracy, Theocracy, Oligarchy, Dictatorship, City State, Socialism, Monarchy, etc. The emphasis in this activity will be not just the building of a society but how it accepts newcomers into its midst. This activity can be a paper-based exercise or expand outward to having students create scale models of a city or community of the future. To do this, however, students must examine existing societal models as part of their research. This may also be realized online through a virtual simulation game. Once completed, the group is required to make a presentation to the rest of the class as a team outlining the details of the project.

Resources

PBS Beyond Brown Lesson Plan
www.pbslearningmedia.org/resource/iml04.soc.ush.civil.brown2/brown-a-landmark-case
www.pbslearningmedia.org/resource/osi04.soc.ush.civil.editorial/ibrowni-reactions-editorials

Collaboration

Students develop an online citizenship project with another school within Canada or around the world to specifically look at areas of immigration, anti-racism and anti-discrimination policies. Members of the group are required to make either oral or written updates concerning the project to the rest of the class.

Resources

ePals
www.epals.com

Current Affairs

Students will examine contemporary examples of citizen engagement and actions around the world where groups have spoken out about racism and developed specific programs or effected certain actions. For example, researching and monitoring the current movements in human rights in African nations, India, Pakistan, Columbia, Chile or Argentina among others. They will also examine the role of the media in this entire process. From this, students will gain insight and a greater appreciation for what they have here in Canada while understanding media influences at the same time. Each member of the group will write a magazine article based on the research they have completed. The article will have a minimum length of one page. The completed articles are then submitted to the teacher for evaluation.

Resources

Human Rights Watch
www.hrw.org

Project Disappeared
www.desaparecidos.org

Office of the High Commissioner for Human Rights
www.ohchr.org

Coming Together

Students working in groups will design and organize a symposium attended by other students in the school and/or community where anti-racism issues are addressed. The outcome of the symposium must be a resolution that features a call to action on the part of the participants. This may also be treated as a class project since it is a large undertaking. The outcome should be the organizing and launching of such an event that may involve other classes, the entire school or the community at large.

Resources

United Nations Association of Canada
www.unac.org

Amnesty International
www.amnesty.org

CULMINATING ACTIVITY

As mentioned at the beginning of this teaching unit, Pier 21 stands as a symbol of welcome for hundreds of thousands who came to Canada's shores years ago. For a long period of time, it was the gateway to the rest of Canada and helped ease the journey for those who were anxious and often afraid.

Working in small groups, students will create their own versions of Pier 21, remembering that it is the symbolic value that is important. So, we're not asking students to design a replica of Pier 21, but to come up with their own concept of how communities can be welcoming, how they can participate in activities to make newcomers within their class, their school, their community feel as if they are part of its fabric. Perhaps, this may mean planning a multicultural festival or special days that recognize different cultures or the staging of a play that explores the welcoming theme. The activity is open-ended but it must focus on the desired result: how to create something (website, video, play, song, poem, demonstration, etc.) that communicates to the community that everyone should be valued and appreciated. Ultimately, the point is to determine what we can learn from each other and how this knowledge helps develop compassion and understanding of those around us.

ASSESSMENT AND EVALUATION

Evaluate each group based on:
- Content (Was the work researched thoroughly?)
- Thoroughness (Was all the criteria met?)
- Effectiveness (Did the group presentations have an impact on the class?)
- Teamwork (Did students work together effectively as a team?)
- Effort (Did students work in a dedicated and cooperative manner, maximizing the talents of the individuals within the group?)

Assess students individually based:
- Knowledge of the issues
- Cooperation, decision-making, and research skills
- Presentation and discussion skills

EPILOGUE

TEACH Magazine delivers hands-on tools and resources directly to teachers. This second volume of The Gold Book of Lesson Plans enables teachers to do what they do best; explore comprehensive themes with students creating a dynamic teaching and learning environment representing the best of 21st century education.

OTHER EDUCATIONAL PROJECTS FROM TEACH:

The Shadowed Road
An exploration of contemporary Ethiopia focusing on global citizenship, human rights, democracy and access to education.

www.theshadowedroad.com

The Ruptured Sky
An exploration of the War of 1812 from First Nations perspectives.

www.therupturedsky.com

80 Degrees North: The Canadian Arctic Expedition 1913–1918
An exploration of a dramatic second, but ill-fated exploration of Canada's North.

www.80degreesnorth.com

Made in the USA
Coppell, TX
05 September 2023